D1070652

Not Til I Have Done

Also by Elizabeth Achtemeier
from Westminster John Knox Press

Preaching from the Old Testament

Nahum—Malachi (Interpretation)

The Committed Marriage

Not Til I Have Done

A Personal Testimony

ELIZABETH ACHTEMEIER

Westminster John Knox Press
Louisville, Kentucky

Book design by Drew Stevens
Cover design by PAZ Design Group
Cover photograph courtesy of Elizabeth Achtemeier

First edition

Published by Westminster John Knox Press
Louisville, Kentucky

This book is printed on acid-free paper that meets the American National Standards Institute Z39.48 standard. ♾

PRINTED IN THE UNITED STATES OF AMERICA

99 00 01 02 03 04 05 06 07 08 — 10 9 8 7 6 5 4 3 2 1

Library of Congress Cataloging-in-Publication Data

Achtemeier, Elizabeth Rice, 1926–
    Not til I have done : a personal testimony / by Elizabeth
Achtemeier. — 1st ed.
       p.   cm
    ISBN 0-664-22136-X (alk. paper)
    1. Achtemeier, Elizabeth Rice, 1926–.   2. Christian biography—
United States.   I. Title.
BR1725.A28A3   1999
277.3'082'092—dc21   98-39672
[B]

For Jean Fenn Farwell

*Former Star of Metropolitan,
Civic, and Light Opera*

Acclaimed Actress

Beloved Friend

Contents

Not Til I Have Done

In chapter 28 of the Book of Genesis, there is a story about the Hebrew patriarch Jacob, who is fleeing for his life. Jacob has cheated his brother Esau out of the inheritance and blessing that should belong to Esau by right as the firstborn son of his father Isaac. Because Esau has vowed to kill Jacob, Jacob is fleeing to Mesopotamia to live with his uncle Laban until Esau's hatred passes.

One day's journey from Beersheba, Jacob camps for the night at a place that he will name Bethel. That evening, as he slumbers, a dream is granted to him of angels descending to earth and of God speaking to him. God gives him the same promise that was granted to his grandfather Abraham. I will give this land to your descendants, God promises. They will become a great nation. Through them I will bring blessing on all of the families of the earth.

God then adds final words to the promise: "Behold, I am with you and will keep you wherever you go, . . . for I will not leave you until I have done that of which I have spoken to you" (v. 15). God will be with Jacob until he fulfills his promise: Not til I have done everything I desire to do through you. Not til my working in your life is complete.

I do not know when I first became conscious of that presence and working of God in my life. I can look back over the years and recall times when I was not granted an opportunity or a position, only to realize later that God had chosen the wiser course for my life. I can remember occasions when I mysteriously sensed that the words I was teaching or preaching were not my words but were being given to me by an Other outside of me. Certainly I can only confess that my marriage was planned by God from the foundation of the earth. Why else did Bud and I suddenly start eagerly seeking one another, when we had been just passing acquaintances for two years before?

God has been at work in my life. I know that beyond all doubt. He has guided its direction, corrected its wayward choices, protected its course, so that I have had to conclude that the promise to Jacob is also partially mine— that God will not leave me until he has done that which he purposes for me.

I also know that is true of each one of you. No one person has a corner on the purposes of God. He created you for a reason, carefully shaping you in your mother's womb, knitting you together with bones and sinews, giving you your unique DNA and fingerprints, your body build and voice, your distinctive characteristics that are like no one else's in the world. The Lord did not do all of that just to ignore you for the rest of your years. No. God planned you unique and unrepeatable because he has a purpose for your particular life. And he will not leave you either until he has done that which he plans for you.

God has a purpose in this world of ours. The scriptures tell us that he is continually working to restore to his creation the goodness that he intended for it in the beginning. The Lord created the world very good. But we human beings, in our self-will, turned it into an evil place full of violence and bloodshed, toil and tragedy, broken relationships, and death. Now God is working to overcome all of that, to restore the love of human community and the loveliness of earth, to bring peace to warring hearts and lives and joy to those in pain and sorrow, to overcome the meaninglessness of death, and to give abundant life eternally. For his instruments in that purpose he chooses us human beings—we who, like Jacob was, are sometimes erring scoundrels; we who constantly wander on our own ways, ignorant of the presence of God; we who mistakenly believe that we are running the world. Nevertheless, the Creator and Sustainer of our lives is there, patiently working with us until he accomplishes in us that portion in his plan for which he made us in the first place.

I did not realize that working of God in my life by seeking something warm and fuzzy, however. I went through all of the adolescent experiences of spirituality that are prompted by countless youth programs—the rallies, the campfires, the discussion groups, dramas and choirs, and Bible lessons. Young people sing and close their eyes and pray earnestly to feel the nearness of God, and some of them do. But it also reminds all of them that there is Someone beyond them named God, and that is a valuable lesson to learn when one is growing up.

But enlightened by my study of the scriptures, I have come to believe that the God who is at work in my life has met me, not so much in the beauty and silence of devotion, but in the routines and disciplines, the joys and disappointments, the encounters and struggles of everyday life. Certainly that is the God who speaks to us through the scriptures. We find him there engaged with the most basic aspects of human existence—with love and marriage and childbirth and death, with the most common relations between neighbors, and with the upheavals and tragedies, the victories and joys of persons and communities and nations.

Perhaps the biblical figure of God the Potter characterizes the Lord of our everydays. God is the Potter, we are the clay, proclaim the prophets (Isa. 64:8; Jer. 18:4, 6; cf. Rom. 9:21). God is working with us to shape us into earthen vessels that can hold the treasures of his gospel, or into cups that can offer someone a cup of cold water in his name. But potters do not *make* pots. They *throw* them! They throw the clay upon a wheel and pound and shape and whirl it. They intimately and carefully mold it with their fingers. They douse it with water when necessary. And from that intimate yet strenuous craftsmanship vessels emerge that can be beautiful and useful and sound.

So too God may pound us and shape us and whirl us about to make us vessels fit for his use. As I look back over my seven decades of life, I believe that is what God is doing with me, and I think that is what he is doing also with you. And that purpose, that pounding purpose of God, is what gives meaning to all our days.

Learning the Faith

No one comes to the Christian faith without the assistance of others. There are many persons who can recount an experience of sudden conversion to belief in Jesus Christ as Lord, which is the basic confession of Christians. But even before that can take place, someone has to tell them at least a portion of the biblical story. Someone has to tell them about Jesus and about at least the principal events of his death and resurrection. Unless we know at least a part of the story, we cannot say, "I believe."

I cannot point to a moment in my life when I was "converted." I grew up hearing the biblical stories and memorizing biblical passages, such as the Beatitudes and 1 Corinthians 13. My earliest recollection is of sitting beside my mother as she explained the biblical story of the picture on the little sheet that I brought home from Sunday school. Many of the pictures depicted incidents from the Old Testament, many from the New. All were reinforced by the stained-glass windows that I could look at on Sunday morning in the First Presbyterian Church in Bartlesville, Oklahoma.

If there was one fact of her life that Mother was determined to pass on to her children, it was her Christian faith. The oldest daughter of a poor Presbyterian pastor of small churches in Ohio, Mother lived and moved and had her being in her trust in Jesus Christ.

She had known a very hard life. She spent her childhood caring for her five younger brothers and sisters while her mother fulfilled the duties and did the good works then expected of a pastor's wife. She worked her way through Wooster College by teaching in one-room schools and by scrubbing floors. She told me that she sometimes was so tired that she would fall asleep while praying on her knees at night. Extremely intelligent and rather serious, she taught in country schools until she married my dad, who was equally poor. Together they scraped through their first years of marriage, as my three older brothers and I were born. But always Mother was undergirded by her faith and her life in the church, and she bent every effort to pass on that life and that faith to us four children.

Mother knew exactly how to go about it. She could be a model for any Christian parent today, for she knew that in the church her children could be exposed to "the means of grace," to the Word of God preached and taught, and to the sacraments of baptism and the Lord's Supper. Through those means, Mother was sure, God would pour out his grace upon us children. Equally, Mother knew that there in the church we could learn the language of faith. We could hear the scriptures read, we could learn to recite the creeds, we could absorb the language of prayer, and we could sing the theology of the hymns.

So we went to church, no excuses accepted. From our earliest years we went to church. My brothers and I would have gladly stayed home to read the funnies or to help Dad in the yard. We were no more eager to go to Sunday school and the worship service than any youngster is. But we went because Mother took us. One of my early memories is of lying on the pew, with my head in Mother's lap, imagining that my hero Tarzan was swinging from rafter to rafter up by the roof of the church building. And I can recall that after a communion service, I had a horrible dream of eating my Sunday school teacher. When I told Mother about it, she carefully explained the symbolism of the Lord's Supper to me, connecting it with the stories of Christ's crucifixion and resurrection.

Certainly the language of the faith that I learned in the church was, above all, comforting. "He Leadeth Me," "The Church's One Foundation," "Breathe on Me, Breath of God," "Love Divine, All Loves Excelling," "Jesus Christ Is Risen Today"—those hymns gradually taught me about God and discipleship and became a part of my own soul and memory.

I loved the music in the church. Perhaps one of the greatest gifts that the Bartlesville church granted me was a choir of outstanding ability. We had a lead soprano who could have sung with credit at the Metropolitan Opera, and our fine choir director had enough sense to hire three other soloists to complement her. As a result, we heard the finest music of the Christian faith, sung incomparably. I learned the scriptures from hearing the *Messiah* and cantatas, requiems, and magnificent chorales. From the first, the Word of God, conveyed through the music, was associated for me with excellence, not to mention sometimes thrilling beauty.

I cannot help but think how impoverished some contemporary worship has become when compared with that music of my childhood and youth. Congregational singing with a guitar and words projected on a screen does not begin to measure up. The words of such music seem to concentrate on us and our emotions. Although the words of a "praise song" may express our feelings, they say almost nothing about God's actions and character. Compare "Father, we praise you; Christ, we praise you; Spirit, we praise you" with "The Church's One Foundation":

> The Church's one foundation is Jesus Christ her Lord.
> She is his new creation by water and the word.
> From heav'n he came and sought her to be his holy
>   bride.
> With his own blood he bought her, and for her life he
>   died.
>
> *(Samuel S. Wesley, 1864)*

A child who learns those words from the earliest years on, and then has them forever in memory, has already been taught something of the biblical story. It was that learning that Mother wanted to instill in her children.

Fortunately, Mother's efforts at educating us in the church were supported by a series of fine preachers in Bartlesville. All of them were graduates of Princeton Seminary, and they preached from the scriptures in those days. We did not hear mere therapy designed to make the congregation feel good, or the nonbiblical opinions of the preacher about some current issues, or the legalistic moralisms that we sometimes hear from the pulpit today. Rather, we heard the Word of God proclaimed, which is living and active and able to transform lives. I learned from those sermons to tell the difference between God's Word and mere human formulations.

We had earnest discussions in the family about the sermons we heard. If a preacher had missed an important point from the biblical text for the day, that was pointed out to us, after Mother—ever the church's gadfly—had already questioned the pastor at the church door about the omission. Mother did not believe that ignorance added anything to the Christian faith. In fact, when I was a student in seminary, she borrowed all of my textbooks to read for herself, and she knew the Bible and basic Christian theology through and through. I learned from the start that faith and the church were to be informed by sound and diligent learning.

I also learned from Mother about the mission of the church. My Aunt Florence was a medical missionary for fifty-five years in India, where she founded a school for training nurses for Mary Wanless Hospital in Miraj. That hospital has now become the only fully comprehensive health-care facility within a 150-mile radius, and serves almost ten million people. Because of my aunt's work, but also because Mother believed that all people should hear the good news of Jesus Christ, she would not let the congregation slack in its mission giving. Every time the budget was voted on at a congregational meeting, Mother took the floor, usually with success, to urge more giving and more support for Presbyterian missionaries. I think I learned at the time from Mother's example not to be timid about speaking out in church meetings and not to be reluctant about calling the plans of the church into question.

The church was the center of Mother's life, and she wanted it to be the center of her children's. Even when we were on family vacations visiting relatives, we went to Sunday school and worship. It was terrible to go into a strange church school class and have all the other children whisper about you, wondering who you were and commenting on your appearance. I rarely heard the Sunday school lesson.

But most terrible of all in my mind was vacation Bible

school, usually a cooperative endeavor by a number of churches that took place early in the summer. I had just been released from school lessons. My shoes had been discarded for the barefoot freedom of summer, my school clothes and books for shorts and play outside. But then I was required to put on a dress and shoes again and to go down to a strange church and listen to women tell Bible stories or make crafts with kids I didn't know. At recess, we had to play ball under a blazing Oklahoma sun, the sweat running down our backs and faces, dampening our very reluctant spirits.

But it took. Through discipline and regularity, through teaching and example, Mother gradually instilled in me the necessity of the church in my life, and through that channel of grace I came to know my heavenly Father and his Son Jesus Christ, whose Spirit has accompanied my life ever since.

Once we know God, however, then we have a responsibility to him, and Mother's child rearing was framed in terms of that responsibility. A petty argument with another girl at school in the third grade brought forth a motherly lesson about forgiveness and the effectiveness of love. Allowance money was to be partly shared with the church. God's love for all people mandated belonging to an integrated group of Girl Reserves, in a time in Oklahoma when the races were strictly segregated. In fact, Mother bore down hard on Christian race relations. She helped sponsor a day-care school for the children of black working mothers. And she helped support the efforts of my Christian paternal grandmother, who moved to the Mexican ghetto across the tracks in order to aid the Mexicans with legal problems about their debts and employment and taxes. Everyday life had set about it a Christian framework, and to that we were held accountable. Indeed, Mother set before her children two scripture verses to guide their growing up: "In all thy ways, acknowledge him, and he will direct your paths," from Proverbs, and "From those to whom much is given, much will also be required," from Jesus' teachings in Luke.

Above all else, Mother prayed for her children. Daily she lifted us up before our heavenly Father and asked his guidance and protection of us. I do not doubt that those consistent prayers of my mother helped shape my youthful years, guiding me in paths that I might not otherwise have taken, steering me away from temptations, supporting me through light and shadow, and encouraging my walk in the Spirit. Ever since Mother died in 1973, my one comfort has been that her Lord, and mine and yours, still intercedes for us all at the right hand of the Father.

You should not think that Mother was an unmatchable parent. There is much that I remember about her that I do not like, and childhood was stormy as well as blessed. But in her unfailing love for her children, her God, and her church, she gave me the most priceless gift I could have inherited—a grounding in the Christian faith from which could grow a lifetime of knowing God. It truly was a pearl of great price, a treasure without price, from whose abundance could come forth the riches that are given in Christ.

On Being Female

I grew up in a neighborhood where there were twenty-one boys, including my three older brothers, and me. It never occurred to me, therefore, that girls couldn't do the same things that boys did. I could field or hit a softball with the rest of them. In fact, in the fourth grade I played on the boys' softball team. The opposing teams from other elementary schools always wanted to know what that girl was doing out in the field. No one on our team questioned it.

I played skate hockey with the boys. We flew kites. We built go-carts. We played games: kick the can, follow the trail, capture the flag, Red Rover. We wandered the neighborhood, the alleys and fields, with no thought in those days that there was any danger facing children who were left to themselves. We had rubber gun battles and snowball fights when blessed with an occasional snow. On the Fourth of July, we awakened every sleeper and scared every dog with whistling tracer bombs and hundreds of firecrackers set off at 6 A.M. Halloween found us all on the streets, our pockets full of gravel for front porches, our Ivory soap ready to cover the windows of any car left inadvertently on the street. In those days, trick or treat was unknown, but we practiced only minor tricks and did not engage in harmful vandalism.

What the neighborhood bunch did, I did, as well as any of the boys. I learned to swim at the age of four, and when the Oklahoma sun drove us to the pool, we all gleefully water-logged ourselves for hours, under water, through the water, in innumerable races and games of tag. I belonged, and no one questioned my status.

Certainly Dad never expected anything different. He had desperately wanted a girl before I was born, and when I arrived he treasured me as a special gift. But he never gave me special advantages, and above all, he never thought there were any limitations set on me because I was female. He figured that if I had brains and worked very hard, I could be anything I wanted to be. Every "A" in school, every prize won, every achievement mastered brought forth his highest praise.

After all, Mother and her mother before her had been college graduates at a time when most women did not go to college. And they were leaders in their churches and communities. They had used their God-given talents to the fullest. Dad expected his children to do the same. After we were grown, he wrote each of us an annual letter inquiring about and assessing what we had accomplished in the past year. He expected us, male or female, to work and to achieve.

In fact, Dad looked down on anyone who was not willing to work hard. When Bud, whom Dad had never met, arrived in Bartlesville two days before our wedding in June of 1952, Dad's first invitation to Bud was to help weed the church lawn. It was a test to see if his future son-in-law was willing to do a menial task all afternoon in ninety-degree Oklahoma heat. Fortunately, Bud willingly passed the test.

With such an upbringing, the assault on the Christian faith by some radicals in the women's movement appeared to me in its beginning as rather silly. Contrary to what is often thought, the women's movement of the last few decades did not start in the 60s. I lived at Union Theological Seminary in New York from 1948 to 1951 with a whole dorm full of women, all of whom expected to play leading roles in the Christian church. I spent the summer of 1950 as an associate pastor and preacher for the Congregational Church at a four-point church charge in rural New Hampshire. I had known many women who had worked to fulfill their ambitions. So when women confined themselves to housework and joined in 1965 in Betty Friedan's published plaint, "Is this all?" I thought, for goodness sakes, of course it's not all! Get out there and use your talents. Stop draining your brains down the kitchen sink.

Indeed, when I have looked at many women of my generation, I have often felt that they constitute an enormous waste of talent in the church. Many of them are intelligent. Many have special gifts and abilities. Many of them are full of the wisdom they have learned as mothers and wives. They have kept the missionary and Sunday school programs of the church alive for years. But their programs in circles and women's groups that have been furnished them by their local churches and denominational head-quarters have rarely engaged their minds or abilities in any strenuous fashion. By not using its women to the fullest, the church for years impoverished itself.

The women's movement has intended to change all that. And indeed, it has had a profound influence on the doctrine, worship, and ethics of the church, much of it beneficial. Females should, indeed, have equal status and opportunities in the life of the church. But when the radical feminists claim that they are "victims," and when they attack the core of the Christian faith by rejecting the Bible and its witness to the nature of God, they undermine the very church they think to improve.

In my forty-seven years of active work in the life of the church, I have rarely met with discrimination. To be sure, there have been a few patronizing clergy. Once when I was asked to preach at the Presbyterian conference center at Massanetta Springs, near Harrisonburg, Virginia, a benighted pastor took twenty minutes before my sermon to set forth his own thoughts because he was sure I had nothing to say. After I preached, however, he apologized for his patronizing. When I first joined the faculty of Union Seminary in Virginia as a visiting professor in Bible and homiletics, a noted Old Testament scholar introduced me to a colleague, who was startled that a female had been employed, with the sarcastic comment, "They get better all the time." Some time later, after the Old Testament scholar read some of my work, he became a friend and freely praised me.

I have preached in hundreds of churches all over the country, and often I have been told after the service, "Well, I never before approved of women preachers, but I guess I have to change my mind."

My usual attitude toward any discrimination directed at me has been just to ignore it and to go on with my work. If you do a good job, your contribution is accepted, whether you be male or female. At least that is true in most of the churches. Sadly, strict and stereotyped nonbiblical doctrine has prevented women from even having a chance to show what they can do in the Roman Catholic Church and among many of the Southern Baptists and Missouri Synod Lutheran congregations. Yet, because of my writing, I have been invited to speak at seminaries of both the Southern Baptists and the Missouri Synod Lutherans, and I have preached at a Catholic mass and taught at Catholic conferences. The door to women has opened a little bit, even in those denominations.

Perhaps my way has been clear in most churches, however, because of the power of the gospel. I have attempted during all of my career to expound and teach and preach the Word of God. And that Word makes its way despite all of the obstacles placed in its path by a sinful society. Jeremiah describes the Word of God as a fire burning in his bones and as a hammer that breaks rock in pieces (Jer. 23:29; cf. 20:9). Bearers of that Word therefore carry with them a powerful weapon—the ability of the Word to make its own way and to change human hearts and minds. Realistically, I have to attribute my unhindered work in the church not to my own ability but to the power of the Word of God of which I am merely a student and servant.

It is for that reason that I have been so alarmed by the course that the radical feminist movement has taken in the church. Its first point of attack was against the language of the church, and again, in the beginning, I thought that was rather silly. I had been raised with all of those hymns that commanded "Rise Up, O Men of God" or that had similar sentiments. I knew, of course, that the hymns also applied to me, a female. That was the way the English language was structured. I took no offense at the usage. But I have been willing to substitute "humankind" for "mankind," to change generic "men" to "men and women," and so forth. Such changes are at least true to the meaning of the biblical text.

But when the radical feminists started changing the language for God, that struck at the heart of my faith.

They wanted to eliminate "Lord," "Father," "Master," "King," but God is all of those—the Lord and King who has ruled my life in love for countless years, the Master whose commands can lead me in the way of life abundant, the Father who sent his only Son to die in order to forgive all my sins and to include me eternally in his joyful household. Those truths about God have been given to me, not by male patriarchal desire to degrade me and to make me a second-class citizen, but by the very speaking of God through his scriptures, in love and mercy and grace. Jesus teaches me to pray "Our Father . . . " He offers me the same relationship that he has with his Father! Should I then turn my back on that fantastic offer of communion, especially since I have come to know that Father of our Lord Jesus Christ?

What sort of God do the radical feminists offer me to replace the Father who has guided me my whole life long? An amorphous something called a Primal Matrix, a Mother Goddess of earth, a Sophia myth, a He/She, a God/ess, an immanent spirit in nature and all persons. They tell me I too am divine with the spirit uniting all things, when I know that is nonsense. They say I have no sin except that of dependence on my Father, a teaching that I can refute with a hundred examples of my wrong. They declare that the cross of Christ was a bloody mistake, an example of the Father's child abuse, when I know very well that sacrifice was the supreme gift of the Father's love for me. They write that there is no eternal life but only absorption back into the goddess, but I know that any deity who cannot defeat death is no god at all. They maintain that recreational sex can be a pathway to God, when I have experienced my faithful oneness with my husband as one of life's highest joys. They say that abortion is every woman's right, but I know it is robbery and killing of a child who has been painstakingly created by God for a purpose.

Everything in my upbringing, my Christian experience, and my years of study of the scriptures has militated against the erroneous path that the radical feminists have taken in our day. So I have opposed their positions in my writing by clinging to the scriptures and to the witness to God given by them. To be sure, there can be a Christian feminism that seeks equal service for women in the church and that has not rejected the biblical revelation of the one true God. But those forms of feminism that have fostered the radical feminists' views have done nothing to further the gospel.

Occasionally, bucking the radical feminist fad has not been easy. Some places where I have been invited to speak have expected a feminist speaker and have expressed their displeasure when I have not fulfilled their stereotyped expectation.

At one seminary, a radical feminist, in the discussion period following my lecture, replaced me at the microphone for thirty minutes. In a few academic communities where the radical feminists rule, my name is anathema. And yet, I have had lots of support. I have received grateful letters, telephone calls, verbal expressions of gratitude from hundreds of women and men throughout the country, because I do not teach and preach about feminist issues. My attempt has been to be simply an evangel of the gospel that I know is true.

Persons everywhere are hungry for the gospel—for the good news that Jesus Christ is risen from the dead and reigns as Lord over all; for the love of God shown forth in that fact, which can forgive our sins and make us new creatures in Christ; for the certainty that the falsehood, the evil, and the violence in our world are not the last word, but that God leads us all toward an eternal kingdom of good and peace and love.

God has directed and led my life along the path of proclaiming those wondrous truths. I can only hope that too has been a contribution to women's lives.

Home and Parents

I grew up surrounded and accepted by boys, but in adolescence the rules change. The hormones start pumping, and suddenly boys are no longer interested in girls who play baseball, but in girls who are pretty. I had lots of friends in junior and senior high school. I edited the school paper and always led my class academically, but I did not have many dates at a time in life when that often determines your status in the eyes of your friends. Adolescence can be a miserable time, though you probably may not realize it at the moment. You have no idea who you are, you're trying to find your niche in life, your body changes, and I, at least, gained weight—lots of weight.

Yet adolescence is also the time when you become interested in talk about God, in what you believe, and in what morals you should have. Because of this interest, any youth leader can engage adolescents in very serious discussion. A dedicated couple in the neighboring Disciples church in Bartlesville took our whole gang under their wing, accompanied us in our activities, let us know we mattered, and gave us opportunity to talk about our faith. Every Sunday night we gathered in the Christian Endeavor meeting at the Disciples church. I can still remember some of those discussions, when the adults simply posed a topic or question and then didn't interrupt. We talked about everything from death to foul language, and it is rather amazing in hindsight to recall the extent to which the young people themselves monitored truth. For example, when we had a discussion about swearing, one fellow remarked, "I don't believe we should ask God to damn anyone." There is a lot of decency in youth who are raised in Christian homes, decency that will manifest itself when given the opportunity of expression.

The church was there when I needed it, because I had been raised in the church. But it was at home that I experienced a turmoil that brought my first taste of real suffering.

Mother and Dad made a handsome couple—Mother with her dark eyes and her hair turned snow-white at an early age; Dad fair-haired, muscular, and erect. But despite the fact that they loved one another, they did not get along very well for many years. In a way, they were two entirely different personalities, and verbal battles were common. Dad had some old-fashioned, stereotyped ideas about how children should be raised: boys should play football; studying music was sissy. So Mother had to fight sometimes in order to let her children live their lives and follow their own interests. Dad was willing to spend thousands in order to buy lovely works of art; Mother thought that was a terrible example of Christian stewardship. Dad loved a good party; Mother was rather shy. Dad was openly affectionate; Mother was reserved, except for the love she heaped upon her children.

Certainly Dad did not object to Mother's devotion to the church. He believed in God, and his Christian sense of fairness, honesty, and humility were respected by all. He was sure that his children should be raised in the faith, and he thought Mother instilled in us worthy ideals. He supported the church financially, but he attended only sporadically. Mother traveled occasionally as a commissioner to synod or presbytery, or as a leader in the Federation of Church Women (which became Church Women United), so when Mother was out of town, Dad made it a point to take us children to church. Otherwise he showed up only on festival occasions like Easter; he was one of those occasional churchgoers who frustrate all pastors.

The quarrels for five years during my teenage years were endless, often terminating in Dad's rage. So Mother and I would go to the Chautauqua Institution in New York State to enjoy its music and recreation during July and August. Finally, in 1940, after many tears on Mother's part, Dad asked for a divorce. At that point, I had to decide which parent I wanted to live with—a decision that no young person should be asked to make. Mother was going to move to Norman, Oklahoma, where we had relatives, Dad would stay in Bartlesville. Mother had made the mistake that no parent should ever make. She had enlisted me on her side in all of the battles with Dad. Yet, in adolescence, one's friends are all-important, and I am sure that I almost broke Mother's heart when I decided to stay in Bartlesville with Dad so I could be near my friends. It was a totally ignorant decision, of course; I could not possibly have existed without my mother. But adolescents are in no position to decide such things rationally.

By the grace of God, however, the divorce never took place. As a Christian, Mother did not believe in divorce, and she was willing to accept suffering for that belief. Dad actually admired and loved Mother very deeply, and he valued his family too much to disrupt its life so drastically. In addition, common concern about two of my brothers, one in the army and one in the navy during the Second World War, bound the folks together. After the war and Dad's retirement, they traveled together and renewed their relationship. Dad even started attending church regularly.

But the turmoil of that adolescent period affected me deeply and, I think, still roils around in my subconscious as a sense of insecurity. Many would say, of course, that Mother should have ended the marriage and avoided the battles; surely, they say, the battles affected me more than a divorce would have. I, however, do not accept such reasoning. Very few children ever want to lose their life with one parent; it is no accident that children of divorce strive mightily at first to reunite their warring parents. God knew our turmoil when he said "I hate divorce" (Mal. 2:16) and when he commanded us, through the prophet Malachi, to avoid such violence. The breakup of a home is violence, nothing less. It does violence to the personalities, the dreams, the plans of everyone involved, and God weeps over the effects that such violence has on all his children.

To be sure, some marriages should be ended—when there is physical abuse, persistent infidelity, resistant alcoholism, or downright cruelty. But as Mother was willing to do, Christians also must be willing to undergo some measure of suffering in order to preserve their homes—just as Christians, in all of their living, are called to experience some suffering. It is not easy to be a Christian in our day and society, but our Lord never promised us otherwise.

In a sense, I am grateful to God for that family experience in my adolescence, and I cannot help but think that God used that time for his ongoing guidance of me. My own turmoil and pain taught me about the suffering that so many persons go through. If we can look beyond our own misery in times of trouble, we come to realize that there is equal misery in the hearts of many around us. We become sensitized to their need. As one lay woman declared at a church conference, "There is a lot of pain out there." I don't think we can fully serve the gospel unless we are aware of that pain.

Certainly God is aware of it. One of the first words he said of enslaved Israel in Egypt was "I know their sufferings" (Exod. 3:7). Jesus, as he hung on the cross, took all of those sufferings upon himself. He knows our pain, our conflicts, our evils, and yes, he knows our death. And the love that reaches out to us in our afflictions is healing and merciful and tender.

Because God is merciful, he also helped me finally in my adult years to appreciate my dad. Throughout my growing years, Dad showered on me a love and care I have seldom seen matched by any other father's love for his daughter. Yet Mother had turned Dad for me into something of an enemy when she enlisted me on her side in my adolescence, and it took me years to get over that terrible, terrible enlistment.

Certainly Mother can be forgiven for such a ploy. My brothers were away at college, and I was one of Mother's few supports. I am sure that the Lord God, in merciful forgiveness, has taken her need into account. Nevertheless, my thinking about Dad had to be reformed, and it was not until adulthood in God's love that I came to appreciate my father. When I became my own person, independent of my parents, I could finally understand Dad as the person he really was, and I was given great admiration for his upright and loving character and for his achievements in his life.

Dad was not an educated man. His father had been killed in an accident when Dad was sixteen, so Dad had to support his mother and three siblings. The consequence was that he never graduated from any school, not even high school. He always had to quit before he graduated and go to work, at first as a janitor. He spent three years as a student at Wooster College, where he waited tables and where he and Mother fell in love. But he could not complete his education there either. Before they were married, Dad took jobs as a low-paid draftsman and as a surveyor and bridge designer for the Santa Fe Railroad.

Dad wanted nothing else than to be a civil engineer, but his engineering training consisted of one year at Washington University in St. Louis, where he crammed in every course he could and paid no attention to the grade he received. On that basis, however, Dad rose to the top of his profession, simply by sheer intelligence and the willingness to study and work hard.

He was hired by Phillips Petroleum Company of Bartlesville as their first engineer, designing natural gasoline plants. The use of natural gas was a new industry, and its manufacture had been primitive at best. But in 1920, Dad designed the first commercially successful gasoline plant, which became a model for the industry for forty years. He rose rapidly through the Phillips company, becoming head of its natural gasoline department, designing the pressurized tanks that made the storage of propane and butane possible, supervising the building of several plants, one of which, the Rice Plant in Borger, Texas, still bears his name. He supervised new methods of transporting several grades of gasoline at once through pipelines, and during World War II he oversaw the building of a thirty-eight million dollar butadiene plant at Borger, which made the manufacture of synthetic rubber possible. In 1949, he received the coveted Hanlon Award as "the outstanding man" in the natural gasoline industry. Given his educational background, his success was simply an amazing achievement, the benefits of which the whole country now enjoys.

I learned something from Dad's successful career, however. A few years after Dad's death, Phillips Petroleum Company published its "66" anniversary volume, but Dad's achievements were not mentioned. His name appeared only once in the book under the picture of the company executives, probably because Dad was not a member of the inner circle of "drinking buddies." It was a testimony to me of the price paid for Christian morality. But it was also a testimony of the fleeting and insubstantial character of earthly fame and fortune. As the psalmist says, "the wind passes over [us,] and [we] are gone" (Ps. 103:16). Few remember what we are or did. Jesus' words are indeed true: "Do not lay up for yourselves treasures on earth, . . . but lay up for yourselves treasure in heaven" (Matt. 6:19–20). For there, with God alone, are found eternal permanence and worth.

Perhaps the same can be said of Dad's hobby, gardening. As in everything else he did, Dad aimed for excellence. So when he and Mother built their home in 1921 at the end of Dewey Avenue in Bartlesville, Dad took two barren lots of earth that had not a tree in sight and turned them into a garden that won Second Prize in the National Gardening Contest in 1934.

Dad loved beauty, so he invested in fine paintings and handsome Navajo and oriental rugs. Most of all, however, he loved natural beauty, and he spread it throughout his town and the whole Southwest, organizing a local garden club, giving away hundreds of plants, supervising the landscaping of high school and church and highways, planting eight hundred redbud trees at the country club, advising his friends what to plant in their yards, and speaking to local garden clubs throughout the Southwest. Even the hundreds of trees in Borger, Texas, are the result of Dad's persuasion of Phillips to plant them so that the workers there would have a nice place to live.

I spent my childhood running and playing in Dad's garden, which abounded in iris and roses. The smell of lilacs perfumed the air, and brilliant goldfish swam in a lily pond. I could sit in the shade of an apple or peach tree or eat strawberries fresh from the picking. The colors of hundreds of daylilies greeted me every early summer; towering pin oaks turned scarlet in the fall; and in winter, evergreens of every kind were draped with the grace of snow. It was an unforgettable gift of good that Dad gave to his children and his city and his region.

I visited that garden five years after Dad's death in 1974, and I found it bare and ruined—the evergreens brown, the roses gone, the daylilies choked with weeds, and two snarling dogs in a cage over the spot where the goldfish had swum in the pond.

The future, for Dad, had always been "next year"—next year when the grass is green again, next year when spring blossoms in beauty, next year when planning and work could add to the loveliness. But as the poet Gerard Manley Hopkins once wrote, there is no key to keep beauty from vanishing away. "The grass withers, the flower fades" (Isa. 40:8), and only three things remain, proclaims Isaiah—the Word of God and the Lord who utters it, and his eternal kingdom (Isa. 51:6).

Human life could be without meaning if we did not have that proclamation, but included in it is the reassurance that God treasures our good. Faith, hope, and love are not lost, wrote Paul, but they abide (1 Cor. 13:13). God takes the little gifts of excellence and hope and faith that we have and the little contributions of beauty and love that we make, and he brings them all to perfection in a kingdom that will not pass away. That is the assurance we have when we remember the transitory past.

Theological Initiation

I started college in 1944, in the middle of World War II. It was considered unpatriotic for civilians to take up seats on long train trips, when so many military men were being transported throughout the country, so instead of beginning my college training immediately at Stanford University in California, I enrolled in the two-year junior Stephens College in Columbia, Missouri. I thereby missed Stanford's two-year course for freshmen and sophomores covering the history of Western Civilization (a course that Stanford now unfortunately has abandoned for reasons of political correctness). Consequently, I can tell you a lot about the history of the ancient Near East in Old Testament times, but my knowledge of the history of the Western world is spotty at best.

Stephens was known as a "finishing school" at the time, and I'm sure Dad hoped I would be "finished." But actually Stephens enrolled some very fine students who were there for the same reason as I. Jeanne Jordon, later to become Jeanne Kirkpatrick, our former ambassador to the United Nations, was in the class ahead of me. Jean Fenn, our class secretary who became my best friend at college, later made her highly successful 1953 debut at the Metropolitan Opera as Musetta in *La Boheme* and sang leading roles in both grand and light opera on three continents.

It is quite true that women's colleges allow females opportunities to develop leadership qualities that they could not have at coed schools. College men tend to judge women by what they look like, and I weighed a hefty 168 pounds at the time, an excess that I later shed at Stanford. But college women judge you by what you are. I was able to participate fully in the student government, an experience that taught me, among other things, how to make a speech in public and how to lead a group.

The religious program at Stephens consisted of compulsory chapel twice a week. I can remember very vividly one chapel talk about our reception of the young men who were coming home without arms or legs from the war, a war that became quite personal for me when Mother phoned the news that the son of our next-door neighbor had been killed in the Battle of the Bulge. I also remember the day that Franklin Roosevelt died and the somber mood that infected the chapel service when we thought about Harry Truman becoming president. Little did we know at the time of the gifts he would bring to the office.

We were a mixed congregation of Protestants, Catholics, and Jews, so the chapel programs centered largely on undefined "values" and "ideals" divorced from any mention of the Christian gospel. Such a program cannot foster growth in the Christian faith. In addition, despite the presence of fine women students, scholastically, Stephens did not give me the best education. My two years there somewhat "marked time" for me and my work.

Stanford University's training, on the other hand, gave me knowledge that has stood me in good stead all my life. I majored in psychology and had courses in all branches of that discipline—among them, child psychology, which was invaluable when I raised my own children; abnormal psychology, which taught me how to recognize mental illness; educational psychology, which showed how people learn; and an introductory course in psychotherapy, which acquainted me with that discipline. In addition, I received the finest training from leading experts in sociology and cultural anthropology; both disciplines have contributed to my writing. I took a course in Great Novels and learned about literary skill, and I continued my love of music with courses in the History of Opera and Wagnerian works.

Like most universities at the time—most of whom have learned better since—Stanford had no department of religion, because their administration apparently did not think religion was important. They at first disdainfully offered only a six-month contract to their campus chaplain, an insulting offer that he turned back to them. Instead, a mystic named Frederick Spiegelberg, a disciple of a writer named Alan Watts, held forth with an eclectic course on world religions that was packed with spiritually hungry students, including me. But I also took a directed study with Spiegelberg that did nothing but study Christian heresies—a wonderful way to learn, not what Christianity is, but what it is not. Because the same heresies occur again and again and still infect the church, it taught me the invaluable ability to separate theological wheat from the chaff.

For some reason that is still a mystery to me, I also initiated student-led Sunday evening vespers in two of the women's dormitories, mixing brief meditations with short recorded classical music, by candlelight. No one asked me to do it; with the approval of the dorm mothers, I just did it. A number of students came each Sunday. Perhaps they too realized that something was missing from their campus life, and vespers gave them a brief recollection of God. On the strength of it, the board of Cap and Gown elected me to their honor society.

Despite the general lack of respect for the Christian faith at Stanford, I had a theological mentor, the campus chaplain Raab Minto, a solid Scotch Presbyterian to whose sermons I listened every Sunday in Stanford's beautiful Memorial Church, and with whom I had innumerable religious discussions. Raab kept my theological thinking on an orthodox, biblical track, and it was he who directed me to seminary at Union Theological Seminary in New York City. Stanford's administration may have thought Raab's ministry was unimportant. For me, it made all the difference for my thinking and for my future.

During the summer after my senior year, I tested out my choice of religious vocation by working in Westminster Presbyterian Church in Pasadena. I quickly learned that my forte was not teaching children in vacation Bible school, but rather teaching adults. I immediately changed my enrollment at Union Seminary in New York from a course of study for directors of religious education to one of preparation for the ordained ministry.

Strangely, I had intended initially to go to Princeton Seminary, as had my future husband, who was still unknown to me and miles away at Elmhurst College. But by the hidden leading of God in my life, we both switched our enrollment to Union instead, and it was there that we met and eventually fell in love. Some would call it chance; I attribute it to God's providence. He has a way of directing our lives when we are least aware of it.

I have always said that from the standpoint of theological education, I was born at the right time, for at Union

Seminary in New York I was confronted by the best theologians in the country: Reinhold Niebuhr in theology and ethics: John Bennett in systematic theology; Paul Tillich in theology; Cyril Richardson in worship; John T. McNeill in church history; Paul Scherer and George Buttrick in homiletics; James Muilenburg and Samuel Terrien in Old Testament; Frederick Grant and John Knox in New Testament; David Roberts in Philosophy of Religion. Union Seminary has never again achieved the theological distinction of having such a faculty, but at that time there was no better place to be grounded in the Christian faith. To that faculty I owe an incalculable debt.

Those men were not only superb teachers, however. They all were also committed Christians and friends. Many of them ate with us in the refectory; often they invited us into their homes; always they were present with us in daily morning worship in the chapel. Niebuhr held monthly freewheeling discussions with students packed into his living room. Muilenburg had an Old Testament study group that met almost weekly in his apartment.

It is difficult to picture the theological intensity that pervaded Union's campus at that time. Every mealtime involved theological discussion, and if you set forth a theological proposition, there was always some fellow student to challenge it or a graduate student to knock it down. There, in those conversations, we hammered out our own positions on the rock of dispute. We learned what could be defended and what was nonsense. Gradually we arrived at theologies that were sound and biblical.

There was no theological professor who was more balanced in his teaching than John Bennett, and it was from him that I learned the essentials of Christian doctrine.

Niebuhr taught us about the pride and sin of human beings in a theological realism that is still perennially pertinent. And I think I never knew truly how to worship until I attended morning chapels with Cyril Richardson and heard his "Amen" booming out at the end of collects, as he prayed on his knees.

We had a lot of fun in the midst of that theological hothouse. One day at lunch we discussed Tillich's theology with Niebuhr. "Tell Tillich," remarked Niebuhr, "that he's a damn pantheist." So off we all scurried to talk to Tillich. Some time later, Niebuhr encountered Tillich in the courtyard, contemplating the flowers growing there. "Paul," asked Niebuhr. "What are you doing?" The reply came back in Tillich's accent, "Ze damn panteist is worshiping."

It always seemed like something of a mental triumph when we managed to wrap our minds around Tillich's system of theology, a system that he simply read to us in class. But try as he might, Tillich could not reconcile his system with biblical theology, and though he had many disciples, most of us faulted him on his distance from the biblical faith. Later we learned about his unfaithful marital life; that simply underscored the weakness in his theology, because a person's theology is made manifest in his or her actions.

Unfortunately, Union chose to waste the knowledge of the brilliant historian John McNeill by letting him lecture only on dates and conditions in church history, whereas to Tillich was assigned the history of Christian thought. Tillich's lecture notes proved totally unusable when studying for the history portion of my Ph.D. exams, because they did not illumine the central traditions of the Christian faith.

Contrary to Tillich's personality, what was impressive about some of the other theological giants at Union was their humility, a humility that we were later to encounter also in Karl Barth. Niebuhr—famous, yet always engaged with students, tall and angular and full of vitality—was never intimidating, but was a beloved friend, and we all wept when he suffered his series of debilitating strokes in the 1950s.

My mentor, my friend, my best teacher at Union, however, was James Muilenburg in Old Testament, and it was because of his inspiration that I took my Ph.D. in that field. Muilenburg began his teaching career as a college professor of English literature, and he had an uncanny ability of immersing himself in the rhetoric and thought of the biblical text. It is no accident that he became a pioneer in rhetorical criticism. When Muilenburg expounded the scripture, the text came alive. God spoke to us through the biblical words; the revelation became ours; and we were set on fire with zeal for the Holy One of Israel.

Muilenburg had a simple method of teaching us the beginning of historical criticism, however. The first assignment we were given in Introduction to the Old Testament was to write a "Pentateuch paper" in which we were required to dig out and explain for ourselves the evidence of multiple sources in the first five biblical books. We had to deal with the duplications, contradictions, differences in style and divine names and theology. After researching that paper, we all knew something of the modern, scholarly approach to the scriptures. We were prepared to begin to learn and to use the tools of modern analysis of texts.

Muilenburg combined for me, and for countless other students who became theological professors, solid scholarship with revelatory insight into the Word of God. There was no more powerful testimony to the faith that I could have received. Nor was there to be found a better teaching model. I have always concluded, therefore, that professors who teach in theological seminaries have not totally fulfilled their calling unless along with their scholarship they have been channels of God's revelatory, biblical Word. The Christian faith is finally "caught," I think; "faith comes by hearing" (Rom. 10:17). Students will hear the faith only as their professors themselves believe and speak it.

I graduated summa cum laude, at the top of my class, and was granted the Traveling Fellowship for study abroad. Mrs. Niebuhr made a big point of saying I had bested all the men, but it didn't seem like such a big deal to me. Dad, however, was ecstatic, and when the *New York Times* carried the headline "Girl Leads Union Seminary Class," Dad bought up all the papers he could find and distributed them to his friends.

Frankly, I had no idea what to do with the Traveling Fellowship. I was terrified to think of studying alone abroad. I stayed at Union one year longer, to begin to fulfill Ph.D. residency requirements, and it was at the beginning of that year that Bud (Paul) and I searched each other out and from then on spent every spare moment together. God has a way of intervening when the need is greatest.

Bud was in the class one year behind me, and the question for us became, Would he too win a Traveling Fellowship and thereby enable the two of us to marry and to study abroad together? When Bud's name was announced as the recipient, our plans were solidified.

We married on my birthday in June at the First Presbyterian Church in Bartlesville, an event not without controversy. A number of Mother's supposed "friends" boycotted the wedding, because Mother was engaged in a civil rights battle of which they did not approve. It seems that the local city librarian had taken three African American women with her to the little all-white Episcopal church on Dewey Avenue. As a result, the city council accused the librarian of being a communist—a frequent charge in the McCarthy era—and fired her from her job. That was too much for Mother. She gathered together a small group of Christians and took the case to court in an effort to have the librarian reinstated in her position. Mother fought the case all the way to the State Supreme Court, but she lost because the city charter mandated that the city council had the right to hire or fire. We all cheered Mother on, however, and we had no regrets about the fact that the segregationists did not attend our wedding. Segregation does not belong in the church.

Bud and I held our wedding reception in the beauty of Dad's garden, and in September we boarded a boat for Europe, the center of theology at the time. It was the beginning of a fantastic adventure.

Newlyweds Abroad

If you turn loose two newly married kids in Europe for two years, they will either meet with disaster or have a ball. Under the protection of a gracious God, the latter was our case.

We discovered that the adventure was a marvelous way to start a marriage. Far away from home and the advice or interference of parents, separated from most Americans, we were totally on our own to work out together all the adjustments and compromises, the changes in habits and learning, that must take place in any new marriage. Fulbright scholarships had not yet begun, so we were practically the only Americans at Heidelberg University. The army was stationed far out of town. We could immerse ourselves in German society.

We spent three introductory weeks at Bonn University in German language courses and then traveled on to Heidelberg. Bud, who had learned some German in his home, became proficient in the language, so much so that he could speak without an accent and consequently had a hard time convincing the Germans that he was American. I on the other hand was illiterate in the language and for weeks existed with a curtain of incomprehension surrounding me. It was so frustrating to hear little German children of three or four years of age jabbering away, when

I, a candidate for a Ph.D., could utter not a word. When we took the train to Heidelberg and stopped at an intermediate station, Bud asked me where we were. I glanced out of the window at a sign and replied, "Bahnsteig," which means "station platform." Such was my ignorance of the language.

As with faith, language is learned by hearing it, however, and Bud wisely sometimes left me on my own to try to make myself understood. We cooked our own meals, and my attempts to buy groceries were stumbling at best. Once I had to describe a pickle—"lang und grün"—in order to buy one at a shop. But because I was trying, the Germans were patient and understanding and more than willing to help.

We rented what had once been a dining room in a third-story apartment in the old city of Heidelberg; we rented it from a kindly widow named Frau Braun, who was sure that "der liebe Gott" had sent us to her. The apartment was what we would call a "cold water walk-up" where from our window we could see the Heidelberg castle up on the hill. There was no hot water and only a basin for washing; after some months I discovered that my sponge baths had missed the back of my knees and they had become black with dirt. The toilet was on a back balcony, where we did not linger long in the winter. Tokens were inserted into a meter to secure gas for the stove. Some of our bedsheets were Frau Braun's old tablecloths.

When we arrived in Heidelberg in October of 1952, coal was still rationed as in the war years, and our room's heat came from a tiny coal-burning stove in the corner. But students could not get a coal card until the beginning of the school year in November. Unfortunately, Heidelberg had one of the coldest Octobers in memory. In order to keep warm, we either snuggled under the huge feather quilt on our bed or went to a movie theater that was heated. Sometimes the theater showed Donald Duck cartoons, and we Americans stood out from the German theater audience when we laughed, because we were the only ones who could understand what Donald was saying! Even when classes started at the university, the lecture rooms were heated only to about fifty degrees, as were also the churches, and it was customary for students to wear their coats to classes.

Germany was still recovering from the war. Everywhere there were ruined buildings, although Heidelberg had never been bombed, because the Allies planned to use it after the war for their military headquarters. Bonn's university library was rubble, however, and when we took a bicycle trip, we sometimes came to cities that had been totally flattened. In one city, on the remaining brick wall of a church someone had written the words in German: "Heaven and earth will pass away, but my words will not pass away" (Mark 13:31).

We were Americans representing the country that had defeated Germany in the war, but never did we experience any hostility from the German people. Frau Braun's husband had been a city official in Heidelberg and had suffered a heart attack as a result of his efforts to satisfy the Nazis. Her son had been taken prisoner by the Allies for three months after the war, because he belonged to the Hitler youth. Yet we were warmly welcomed by her and the other Germans, I think for three reasons. First, we were in the country, not as conquering Americans but as students immersing ourselves in the language and culture. Second, we were poor. My Dad sent us $100 every month, and we lived for two years on that, plus our $2400 of scholarship money.

For desserts after our meals, we often went to a candy shop and bought fifty grams of hard candy, which we then meticulously divided between us. After a while, the shop-keeper would greet us with "Guten Abend, Herr und Frau fünfzig Gramm." ("Good evening, Mr. and Mrs. fifty grams.")

Most notably, however, we were welcomed by many Germans because we were Christians. Frau Braun held weekly prayer meetings with women neighbors in her living room, and every Sunday morning she shared her newly baked breakfast cake with us. Once we accompanied German students on an evangelistic week to a small German farming village. There in the home of a crippled widow we learned that she had been wounded and that much of her house, including her precious pump organ, had gone up in flames from American bombs. The village had suffered attack because the flares dropped before the bombing over the industrial city of Karlsruhe had drifted on the wind over to the little farming village. Although resentment toward us could have been understood, that widow prayed with us and, when we left, offered us the only gift she could give in her poverty—two fresh eggs from her hens. Such experiences everywhere taught us a lot about the power of the Christian gospel to transcend boundaries of nationality and to overcome former hatreds.

During one university vacation, through the World Council of Churches, Bud secured us the opportunity to live and work for a month in two refugee camps in northern Germany that were way stations for children under fourteen years of age who were crossing over into the West before the Berlin wall was built. The camps, with their rough bunkhouses, during the war had served as prisons for political prisoners. Bud worked in the camp for boys, I in the camp for girls a few miles away. Bud would come over to visit me only on the weekends.

Most of the youths who passed through those camps had fled with only the clothes on their backs when their parents had been arrested by the Russians. One fourteen-year-old, who had lost an eye, had hitchhiked all the way from Poland. The young people often told tales of coming home from a youth meeting at church, only to find their parents gone, their houses empty of loved ones. Once, as I was walking to church with a group of the girls, one of them suddenly started sobbing in the middle of a sentence and then quickly regained her composure.

All of the youngsters were waiting for placement with relatives or someone who would guarantee their support in other parts of West Germany. During the one or two weeks that they were at the camp, some of them sewed, some found clothing in the huge pile of cast-off clothes sent from the United States, most of them simply talked and waited anxiously for reassignment. Their greatest fear, however, was that they would not be reassigned to a relative they knew because that particular German district already had its quota of refugees. Their second greatest fear was that there were spies among them; they had experienced far too much tyranny. From me they wanted English instruction and above all to learn the latest popular songs. With Bud the youngest boys played innumerable games of cards and taught him German slang. I often wonder what became of them and whether they have been able to experience some normality in their lives.

At Heidelberg University, I studied with the noted Old Testament scholar Gerhard von Rad. Bud had classes with Edmund Schlink and Peter Brunner. Everyone spoke

German, of course, and I finally gained enough facility to take all my lecture notes in that language. In one sense, it was a year preparing us to go on to the university in Basel, Switzerland, to study with Karl Barth, Walther Eichrodt, and Oscar Cullmann.

At the end of our year in Heidelberg, however, we set out on a bicycle trip that would take us the eight hundred miles from Heidelberg to Copenhagen. There were very few cars on the road. Germans too were traveling by motorcycle or bike, often sleeping overnight in farmers' barns. For the most part, we stayed in tiny guest houses for pennies a night, carrying our own food and cooking it beside the road on a small portable gasoline stove. Our boast became that we had eaten in some of the best ditches in Deutschland. We avoided the youth hostels as much as possible, because most of them were filled with little German boys who talked half the night and told a lot of dirty jokes. After riding for about thirty miles a day, we just wanted some sleep.

We never knew where we would stay at night. We just rode as far as we liked. One evening we found ourselves far from any lodging, but a farmer directed us to the lodge of a group known as Naturfreunden ("Nature friends"). There we were directed to put our sleeping bags beside many others on a long wooden shelf in a large upper room of the lodge. To our amazement, everyone, male and female, then proceeded to undress for bed. We shed our clothes *inside* our sleeping bags and got dressed the same way the next morning. At times children would gather, full of questions, as we ate beside the road. Once, the local drunk passed by with a whole line of children marching behind him.

We had a few mishaps. A flat tire would send Bud into a town to get a replacement. When it rained, we donned ponchos and stopped occasionally to clean the water off of our eyeglasses and to wring out our socks. Or we took refuge under the eaves of a barn until the rain slacked off.

For most of the trip, we followed lovely river valleys that avoided the hills. Occasionally, we loaded our bikes into a boxcar of a local train in order to bypass some particularly difficult terrain, a practice that traveling Germans were also employing. But we were healthy; we got an intimate view of the German countryside, along with its ruined cities; and we encountered nothing but friendliness from the population.

When we passed into Denmark, the people there did not want to hear German spoken (the same was true later in Holland), so usually they would ferret out some citizen who spoke English and who could give us directions. Copenhagen became our favorite city, and we had a glorious time touring it on our bikes, eating Smørbrød in its lovely parks and going to its wonderful amusement park, Tivoli, in the evenings. In addition, a kindly Danish woman, who had just built a new apartment house, turned over the whole top floor of that building to us, let us store our bikes and luggage there, and kept them safe for us while we went on to Sweden to tour through the Göteborg canal. Only on that boat trip did we meet any unfriendliness—from rich Americans who were sure that we, in our biking clothes, were lowering the tone of their luxury cruise. They all got seasick when the boat passed across a large stormy lake; we sat on the top deck and lustily sang, "Blow ye winds, hi ho!"

Our intention after visiting Sweden and Denmark was to ride our bikes back across Jutland (northern Denmark), down through Holland and Belgium, along the Rhine to Heidelberg, and thence on to Basel, Switzerland. As we pedaled through northern Denmark, however, we were met by driving rain and headwinds that turned our ponchos into sails that pushed us backwards. It was clear that we would be exhausted, so we traded in our bikes for two one-cyclinder mopeds (motorized bicycles) and went merrily on our way at about fifteen miles per hour. For the next year, all during our time in Basel, that became our mode of transportation.

Switzerland had been a neutral country during World War II, and the citizens were very proud of it, although we wondered at the time if one should be proud of selling fine machinery to Adolf Hitler. Had they opposed Nazism, they would have immediately been overrun, of course, even though every man under sixty years of age was a sharpshooter and trained in the Swiss army. The Swiss probably could have withstood any troops for months from rock bunkers that they had dug deep into their mountains. We even heard that Barth took great pride in the fact that he was a private in the Swiss army during the war and had been assigned the post of guarding a bridge!

Switzerland had always been portrayed to us as an ideal democracy, so it came as a shock to learn that the women could not vote. Indeed, under a strict civil regime, Basel largely ignored its women. When we went to the officials to register—for our presence as well as our radio had to be recorded—every question about my age, citizenship, and occupation was addressed to Bud, despite the fact that I was standing right beside my husband. My answers were invalid; the men answered for the women. It took years for female suffrage to occur in Switzerland, because when the men in each canton were asked to vote on whether women should be given the vote, the men invariably said no.

We rented a room in the home of Professor Fritz Buri, who was known at the time as a radical liberal. Barth remarked, when he inquired about our housing, that perhaps we were put there for missionary purposes. The Buris had two children, plus a live-in young maid of about seventeen who got up every morning at 5:00 A.M. to kindle the coal stoves scattered throughout the house. When we wanted to take a picture of the whole group, including the maid, the Buris were incensed that we included their servant. Nevertheless, they were most kind to us personally, allowing us to use their kitchen facilities and to wash our clothes in their ancient washing machine in the water they had first used for theirs!

During a month's vacation from the university, we bought a ticket for $15 that would allow us to travel on a train, third class, from the border of Switzerland to Sicily. The only provision was that we remain six days on that island. If you have ever traveled third class on an Italian train, you know it is a wild ride, with people getting off and on, not through the doors but the windows. Italians, the friendliest people in the world, wanted to talk to us, so the conversation in our compartment was incomprehensible but gaining steadily in volume—the idea being that if you talk louder, perhaps you can be understood. But then the Italian man beside Bud in our compartment discovered that Bud knew Latin, and the man knew the Latin mass. After that, the "holy language" became the means of converse, and the Italian took it upon himself to explain transubstantiation to Bud. The virgin Mary, he said, was walking down the street one day, carrying the baby Jesus in her arms. When Herod approached her, however, the infant turned into a bouquet of flowers, but then turned back again into Jesus after Herod had passed. Presto! Transubstantiation!

We stopped in Rome and Naples on our way down Italy. In Rome we toured the forum, of course, but were given the willies by dozens of fierce-looking stray cats who eyed us hungrily as we ate our lunch. In Naples, we learned what poverty in the Mediterranean world looks like. People were living there in caves dug into the sides of hills, and beggars were everywhere on the streets. We gave to a few of the latter, but I will never forget the woman who approached us with outstretched hand while a small boy and girl clung to her ragged skirt. Her face was full of desperation, but we had little money and could not give again. I have had the feeling ever since that I was confronted by my Lord in that beggar woman that day and yet passed him by.

After six lazy days in Sicily, we came back up the Italian peninsula, stopping at Taromina with its hundreds of flower gardens, visiting the loveliness of Venice, which had not yet begun to sink, and standing overawed by the thousands of treasures of art in Florence. But it was in Basel, with Barth and our student colleagues, that we encountered the greatest treasure.

Karl Barth and the Word of God

In contrast to our year in Heidelberg, there were many Americans studying theology at the University of Basel, and we became part of a unique group of young theological students, most of whom would go on to theological professorships in our country's seminaries and divinity schools: Brevard Childs, Shirley Guthrie, Paul van Buren, James Wharton, John Deschner, and the British David Torrance. It was a group with whom we had endless stimulating and enlightening theological discussions.

What drew us all to Basel was a slightly plump, rumpled, gray haired, middle-aged man who could have been anyone's grandfather—Karl Barth. In fact, one colleague reported that when he and his small child met Barth on a walk, Barth got down on one knee and said "woof woof" to the child in an attempt to elicit a smile.

Similarly, Barth could have been anyone's beloved pastor, because he fulfilled that role in relation to his students. He was interested in how we were faring in his country, inquiring about our living arrangements, our adjustments to living abroad, our families, our views, and our youthful interests. He welcomed one-on-one conversations with his students. When Bud talked with Barth in his study one Saturday morning for an hour and a half, Barth thanked Bud for the discussion. At the end of our year, he accompanied all of us in his English-speaking seminar down to a local wine cellar for conviviality and theological talk. We learned at the time that Barth not only had a consuming interest in the American Civil War, but that he also liked to read detective stories and accounts of UFOs. We asked him if it would change his theology if life were discovered on another planet, to which he replied, "Und wie!" ("And how!"). One of Bud's prized possessions is a picture of himself sitting next to Barth at that restaurant table.

Barth also had a twinkling sense of humor, and innumerable stories circulated about him. One told of the day when Barth walked down to the trolley stop to board the car; he took a seat beside a local man. As the trolley went back up past Barth's house, the man remarked, "That's the house of the famous theologian, Karl Barth. Do you know him?" "Know him," Barth replied, "I shave him every day!"

Yet this was the man who changed the shape and content of theological knowledge throughout the world; he was the "Luther" of our time who undermined nineteenth-century theology and set theological disciplines on a new course. Unfortunately, since Barth has died many theological and biblical studies have thought to reverse that direction and to return to the nineteenth century, relying once again on subjective feeling and eliminating transcendence from the scriptures.

We took several courses with Barth, as well as courses with Eichrodt and Cullmann. All of us sat in on Barth's general lectures in which he simply read to us from the next volume of the Church Dogmatics, putting in the commas and making corrections as he proceeded. That would not qualify with many as a way to teach, but there was nothing dull about it. Barth set forth the implications of the Word of God in all of its power and authority, and I had the feeling that we were listening, not to a lecture, but to a revelation of the living God.

Bud took a seminar on Calvin with Barth, and we both sat in on his seminar that was going carefully through the document *Jesus Christ the Hope of the World*, which was to be the centerpiece of the upcoming World Council of Churches Assembly at Evanston. We later heard, when we had returned to this country, that at a preparatory conference for that Assembly, Niebuhr dismayed Barth by terming eschatology irrelevant. For Barth, such a stance was incomprehensible, because the scriptures are full of eschatology.

Both of us also were participants in Barth's English-speaking seminar where the Church Dogmatics were discussed. Barth remarked at the time that had he known English was going to become the lingua franca of the theological world, he would have learned it a little better. He spoke excellent accented English, however, had no difficulty expressing his thoughts, and was very easily understood. In that seminar we had the opportunity to discuss particular points in Barth's writing.

When we initially journeyed to Europe, Bud had the intention of earning his doctorate in systematic theology, but his time there convinced Bud that he could not be a theologian without thorough knowledge of the New Testament. He therefore switched his major to that field and has been a New Testament scholar ever since. Unfortunately, much theology under construction today has almost no connection with the scriptures and therefore has very little claim to Christian truth, because the one true God reveals himself to us through the witness of Israel in the Old Testament and, supremely, through the testimony to Jesus Christ in the New Testament.

My field was Old Testament, of course, and what Barth did for me was to confirm and deepen what I had learned thus far in biblical study, because Barth's theology emerged from the scriptures and had the scriptures always as its base.

Barth set forth the Word of God incarnate in Jesus Christ. All truth emerged from that center, and all was responsible to it. The Word for Barth was the Word that the apostle Paul also spoke: "the power of God and the wisdom of God" (1 Cor. 1:24), the power unto salvation. In short, the Word is not static truth, not religious principle, not new idea, but the active working of God within human life. That is exactly the understanding of the Word of God that one finds in the Old and New Testaments. From the beginning of Genesis on through the Bible, the Word is the active, effective force that creates new situations: "Let there be light" (Gen. 1:3). "If any one is in Christ, he is a new creation" (2 Cor. 5:17). The Word accomplishes that which it speaks: "My word . . . that goes forth from my mouth . . . shall not return to me empty, but it shall accomplish that which I purpose, and prosper in the thing for which I sent it" (Isa. 55:11). The history of salvation confessed in the scriptures is a history moved forward, shaped, guided by that almighty Word.

The Word of God is given us, furthermore, not by the wisdom of human beings, not from the learned disciplines of earth, not from human conscience or observation, and not from the world of nature: the wisdom of God is foolishness to humankind and is "what no eye has seen, nor ear heard" (1 Cor. 2:9). The Word is spoken by the God whose ways are not our ways and whose thoughts are not our thoughts (Isa. 55:8). God is holy God; that is, he is totally other than anything or anyone in all creation. Thus the Word incarnate in Christ must be revealed to us through revelation, through the Spirit that is from God—coming from outside of us yet mercifully poured into our hearts. Through the scriptures of the Old and New Testaments, the trinitarian Spirit speaks, revealing the nature, the will, the goal of the God and Father of our Lord Jesus Christ. Barth could therefore write in his little book *Homiletics*:

> The gospel is not in our thoughts or hearts; it is in scripture. The dearest habits and best insights that I have— I must give them all up before listening. I must not use them to protect myself against the breakthrough of a knowledge that derives from scripture. Again and again I must let myself be contradicted. I must let myself be loosened up. I must be able to surrender everything. (*Translated by Geoffrey W. Bromiley and Donald E. Daniels [Louisville: Westminster/John Knox Press, 1991], 78*).

It follows, therefore, that all valid religious insight comes not by moving from the human situation to God, but by beginning with God and moving to the human situation. We are not to begin with human rights or experiences or needs and then expect God to be accommodated to them. Rather, we are to begin with what is biblically revealed by God's actions and words, and on that basis understand human vicissitudes and minister to them. That is the stance in which the scriptures are in fact the authority for faith and life; that is the movement that characterizes a truly biblical worldview.

In contrast, much of contemporary American theology, with its reliance on subjective feeling and experience, is indeed foolishness, the futile attempt once more to create our own truth and thereby to make ourselves into our own gods and goddesses. Similarly, contemporary American deconstructionism, which maintains that there is no truth and that everything is relative to the individual, has never known the objective Word and its power that comes not from within us but from without—from God.

With his emphasis on the objective power of the Word of God and its ability to create newness, Barth has often been criticized in homiletical circles for ignoring the congregation in his preaching—for not trying to establish some connection with the lives of the people listening, but rather simply relying on the power of the preached Word to make that connection. That criticism begins to be undermined when we realize that much of Barth's preaching was carried on for prisoners in the Basel jail. Barth took very seriously Christ's words in Matthew 25: "I was in prison and you came to me" (v. 36). When he was in this country, Barth insisted on visiting Chicago's prison. A number of his prison sermons are collected in a little book called *Deliverance to the Captives* (London: SCM Press, 1961), but it was the prisoners themselves who loved Barth so much that they first printed that book.

Criticism of Barth's homiletical method is further undermined when we read the sermons in that book. Consider the following excerpt from a sermon entitled "Death—but Life," based on Romans 6:23: "For the wages of sin is death, but the free gift of God is eternal life in Christ Jesus our Lord." It was preached to the Basel prisoners on Easter Sunday, 1959.

Death is called here "the wages of sin." It could also be called the pay, the salary, the compensation paid by sin to those who are in its service and work for it. Strange, isn't it? Sin fulfills here the function of the paymaster in the armed services, or of the employer or his cashier in a business enterprise who pays the employees and workers. Here is what is your due, what you have earned through your efforts. Is it the correct amount? Take a good look! Absolutely correct, isn't it ? (p. 146). . . . Eternal life is the free gift of God. It is not the wages, the salary, the compensation, as death is the wages of sin. Eternal life is not our due from God. It is nothing we have earned. It is not a payment for services well done. Eternal life is not the grand total at the bottom of the payslip . . . . God is no paymaster or employer or cashier ready to settle accounts. God does not settle accounts. God is a very distinguished gentleman whose privilege and enjoyment is to give freely and to be merciful. (p. 148)

Perhaps the best thing one can say about Barth's preaching is that, with simple illustrations such as those used in the above sermon excerpts, he preached the Word of God. The principal content of his sermons was not human problems but God's actions—a characteristic that marks all outstanding preaching. His intention always was to make that Word clear to educated and uneducated alike. He achieved that clarity with his skillful use of everyday illustrative material that spoke to the hearts of his listeners. Would that all preachers would do the same!

The treasure of great price that we were given in Basel was the Word of God in Jesus Christ set forth in all of its power and purity. That has been a gift that has undergirded and directed my life ever since.

When we left Basel for our journey homeward, Bud and I stopped in London, rented a tiny car, and drove up the eastern coast of the British Isles to John o' Groat's and then down the westward coast through the lake country and Wales, visiting the many cathedrals, Stratford-on-Avon, and other historic sites. We also had fun stopping at little pitch-and-putt courses to rent clubs and play golf, although when we played standard courses, Bud had words for the rocks and undergrowth that characterized the rough on Scottish golf courses. "That's not rough," he exclaimed, "that's suicide!"

We discovered on that trip that I was pregnant with our first child, and though I had no morning sickness, I longed for good food. The only thing that sustained me each day, as we ate our lunches beside the road, was the expectation of eating hearty British breakfasts every morning. When my parents met us in London and we gave them the news of my pregnancy, Dad remarked, "Well, that's that," thinking that my days of study and career were over. But of course, that was not that at all.

We went back to Union Seminary in New York to complete the work on our doctoral degrees: Bud on the difficult Th.D. from Union; I on a Ph.D. from Columbia University—a degree worked out jointly with Union, which did not give Ph.D.'s at the time.

I served as a teaching assistant to Muilenburg, grading his papers and occasionally leading a seminar session. I graded the Pentateuch papers written by Phyllis Trible and Frederick Buechner. Even then, Buechner's prose was remarkable. His discussion of the Yahwist source in the Pentateuch was a literary delight.

I took my eight-hour general exam for my Ph.D. from Columbia when I was seven months pregnant with our son, Mark. Three years later I took the rigorous exam on my dissertation, which dealt with righteousness in the Old Testament; at the time I was eight months pregnant with our daughter, Marie. I think the religion department of Columbia University thought I was perpetually pregnant! Both exams were very tiring but successful experiences. My doctorate was awarded me in 1959. Bud had received his, dealing with salvation history in Romans, in 1958.

❖ ❖ ❖ ❖ ❖

Combining Career,
Marriage, and Children

Our son Mark was born in New York City in 1955 while I was a teaching assistant for James Muilenburg and two months after I took my eight-hour field exam in Bible for my Ph.D. It is not difficult to find study time when a child is an infant because the child sleeps so much. But after Mark's first birthday, we occasionally called on Bud's mother to come and entertain Mark while I studied. She was more than willing to help and was wonderful with little children. Bud, however, had to postpone his New Testament field exam for six months, because he was responsible for Mark's 11:00 P.M. feeding. And there was one time when I had to call Bud out of a graduate seminar session, because he was the only one who knew how to make Mark's formula!

Once our residency requirements and initial exams were successfully completed, Bud accepted a call to Elmhurst College in 1957 to teach in its religion department. We stayed in Elmhurst only one year, because on the day that Bud began teaching there, he received the call to become a New Testament instructor at Lancaster Theological Seminary in Pennsylvania. Seminary teaching was always his goal, and we excitedly accepted the move to Lancaster and remained there for the next sixteen years. There our daughter Marie was born in 1959, and when she was three months old, Robert V. Moss, the seminary's president, invited me to teach Old Testament theology as a visiting professor.

Lancaster had a rather amazing faculty during our initial years there. Reinhold Niebuhr once characterized it as a quiet little Evangelical and Reformed seminary, but among our colleagues on the faculty were David Steinmetz, Gabriel Fackre, and Bard Thompson for one year, all of whom went on to distinguished professorships in other seminaries, plus the Hungarian Bela Vassady, accomplished librarian George Bricker, and the Roman Catholic Jesuit Bill Walsh, whose piety endeared him to all of the students. It was a stimulating group.

Many women these days struggle with the question of whether or not it is possible to combine an academic career with their roles as mothers and wives. Speaking from my experience, I can affirm that it is. We were blessed by the fact that we lived close to the seminary and could schedule our classes in such a way that one of us was always home with the children, so that we did not need to turn their upbringing over to babysitters or nursery schools. To be sure, Mark still maintains that while I was finishing my Ph.D. dissertation he took the longest naps of any kid in the neighborhood. He considered it a minor triumph when he learned to crawl out of his crib and then taught his little sister to do the same. But we, not someone else, raised our children.

I have always held that my call to the Christian ministry includes my call to be a wife and a mother, and I cannot neglect one part of that call for the other. Someone asked me one time at a conference where I was speaking, "What is the most significant thing you have ever done?" I had no hesitation in answering, "I helped raise two wonderful children." Although I suppose I have taught many students how to preach and have sometimes opened the Bible and especially the Old Testament to clergy and laity alike, I am sure that I have exercised more influence on the world through those two children than through anything else. Both of them are fine Christians, married to equally fine Christian spouses; they are active in their churches, are teaching the gospel and raising their five children in the Christian faith. And those five grandchildren of ours will in turn go on to teach the next generation. So the good news of Jesus Christ will be spread.

There are other considerations that I think should be kept in mind by any woman who aspires to both a career and marriage and children, however. My course was made possible only by the full support and cooperation of the husband whom God sent to me. When we were first married, I wondered if I should continue my doctoral work; but Bud said that was the best life insurance we could have, because if something happened to him, I would be qualified to support myself and the children.

We learned rather early in our marriage that although we were both in the biblical field, we were not competing with each other. Rather, we were encouraging each other, and as we have developed in our respective fields, we have supplemented each other. It's a great thing to have your own New Testament expert sitting at the dining room table with you! At the same time, Bud sometimes asks me information about the Old Testament. When we first started writing books and articles, we often submitted them to each other to read. I always figured that if I could get something past Bud's expertise, I could get it past any editor. Now in our later years, we know each other's thoughts so well that the mutual check is not necessary.

If one has a call to marriage and motherhood as well as to an academic pursuit, one also has to make choices, sometimes hard choices, that will honor both sides of the call. I have been a visiting or adjunct professor all of my life, which position carries with it very little money and not much status in the eyes of outsiders, although to my mind my life couldn't be better. Once, after we were situated at Union Seminary in Richmond, we were both invited to become professors at Pittsburgh Theological Seminary. Bud, who was already a full professor, unselfishly said, "If you want to go, we'll go." I had no desire to go. Similarly, I was invited by Duke Divinity School to be its homiletics professor, spending three days each week in Durham, North Carolina. Again, I said no, because I did not think it would be beneficial for our marriage. The happiness we have known in our years of married life has more than vindicated those decisions.

If a woman wants both a career and a home, however, she must also realize that it takes planning and scheduling. I never have been able lazily to waste time. Bud and I have a saying that "you can't sit around the house and read magazines and eat bonbons." You can't spend hours in front of the TV. You must plan what you are going to do when, and you must do it. Yet my life has been full of many interests: gardening and tennis, boating and swimming, sewing and reading, and hours spent in recreation with Bud. We have always smiled a little when we hear someone say, "I have a book I want to write, but I can't find the time." There is time enough for all if there is the will to plan and do.

After we spent the summer of 1958 in humid, hot, and steamy Lancaster, Pennsylvania, we determined to build ourselves a summer cabin somewhere on a lake in the state. We both love the outdoors and sports, and we wanted our children to know something besides city life.

We took out a map and wrote to every Chamber of Commerce in a Pennsylvania town that was situated near a lake. Some replied that no lakefront property was available. One place we visited turned out to be a flood-control dam with a puddle. But finally we located property on the north shore of Lake Wallenpaupack in the Poconos.

Bud stayed awake for hours one night, agonizing over whether we could afford the property and the cost of putting up a modest cabin. Finally he decided that if someone else could build a house, so could he. So we had the builders put up the cabin shell with the plumbing and electric outlets—"the largest outhouse in Pennsylvania," Bud called it. Then for the next sixteen years, Bud finished that cabin inside and out, even making the furniture. He said he thought he had good New Testament precedent for being a carpenter. Each summer we bought only the amount of lumber we could afford. My birthday present one June was the shower stall and kitchen floor. We lived summer to summer with what was finished. I gradually built the stone walk, patio, and walls outside.

But that small cabin in the forest, beside Lake Wallenpaupack, became a permanent home to our children, and each summer they have returned to it with their families. There they learned to swim, row a boat, and sail. They learned to fish and hike, and Mark learned how to find his lost way out of a forest, using a compass. They saw raccoons and foxes, bears and woodchucks and deer. The animals we encountered in those woods presented us with countless tales.

Once, an elderly man who lived next door to us was met by a large raccoon that came up the path and sat up in front of the man. The animal had a barbed fishhook in its lip and was asking for help. Quickly, the old man ran into his house, got a pair of pliers, donned gloves, and then carefully cut loose the fishhook. For weeks afterward, the raccoon came to visit and to eat the loaf of bread that the man gave him. Another time, I baked a pan of brownies and carried it out to the screened front porch to cool, only to discover a full-grown black bear sniffing the aroma at the front door. Fortunately, the bear was not hungry enough to break through the screen.

That summer place was a paradise that drew our family together for two or three months every summer. Having the experience, we could never understand why some parents want to take either separate vacations or vacations without their children. Our joy was in our togetherness as the children grew toward college years and adulthood.

Parents can give their children only limited gifts. We could pass on our faith and life in the church to them. We could give both of them good educations: Mark has a Ph.D. from Duke Divinity School; Marie a Doctor of Laws from the University of Virginia. We could give them unconditional love and a firm sense of right and wrong and self-discipline. But parents can also give children one of the most important things in their life—a happy home.

Bud and I have long known that the basic ingredient of a happy marriage is lifelong commitment—hence my most popular book, *The Committed Marriage*, which was published in 1976 (Philadelphia: Westminster Press). I wrote that book because every other book that I read on marriage regarded faith simply as a final chapter added on to all the other requirements for a good marriage: communication, agreement about money, a good sex life, and so forth. But the Christian faith is not just an appendix added on to the main subjects; it is the framework and context of the entire marital relation.

The scriptures tell us that Christian marriage is to be a mirror, a reflection of Christ's relation to his church (Eph. 5:32). That means that our relation to our spouses is to have the same lifelong faithfulness that our Lord has shown to us. Jesus never says to us, "I will love you until someone better comes along," or, "I will love you if you fulfill all my needs." No. He promises us, "Lo, I am with you always" (Matt. 28:20). That is the promise that is encompassed in Christian wedding vows: "to have and to hold from this day forward, for better for worse, for richer for poorer, in sickness and in health, to love and to cherish, till death us do part." In short, no matter what happens to us, I will be there. No argument will break our covenant. No change in circumstances will destroy our bond. No ill fortune will cause me to leave. Through all the vicissitudes of our years, we will remain together. The sense of freedom to be one's self, to communicate one's inmost thoughts and desires, and to know security in sharing the richness of life is given by that commitment. It lies at the center of those happy homes in which children grow and flourish.

Having made that commitment, married partners of course must know how to forgive as our Lord Christ has forgiven his church, for disputes, sins, errors, selfishness mark even Christian marriage. Forgiveness involves forgetting as well, so that past hurts and grudges are not stored and hauled up when a new difficulty arises. From parents' forgiveness of one another, children learn how to forgive and are taught that disputes can be healed by forgiveness's mutual love.

Christ pays very close attention to his church; he knows each individual's path and person. So too Christian marriage partners are attentively to know one another, making time for the other's presence, seeing and listening to the loved one. In Thornton Wilder's profound play *Our Town,* the daughter complains, "We don't have time to look at one another" (New York: Coward McCann, 1938. third act, p. 124). Far too often that is the situation in modern homes, especially those in which both spouses are pursuing a career or job. But we are to see one another, to note when the other is tired or perhaps has cut a finger, to make time for being with one's spouse even if one's own activity is disrupted. Taking time, noticing, listening is part of what it means to "honor" one's spouse. These actions bestow a dignity and importance—a "weight," the Bible would call it—apart from which individuals are turned into nonentities. Certainly, for children, the ability to honor others is part of being civilized.

Marriage can be a power struggle or it can be a mutuality, and that shared power of decision and shared service is the model the scriptures hold out to us. "Be subject to one another out of reverence for Christ" (Eph. 5:21), they tell us, which involves not pride but humility, the willingness mutually to serve one another and to relinquish pride of first place, with first one and then the other leading and deciding. Unless a marriage achieves that mutuality, one of the partners is going to be unhappy. And unless children are taught that service of others, they can never know what it means to be Christian.

Christian marital partners never go it on their own, however. They are supported and guided by the love of Christ, who works with us, not only as individuals or as a church, but also as married couples. In his sacrificial love and forgiveness, and attention and ministry to our every need, we find a strength and a guidance far beyond our own capacities. I have no doubt that Jesus Christ has supported and guided the course of my marriage. I also have no doubt that he will support and guide any couple who turns to him in trust.

I also have no doubt that Christ has protected and guided our children, in answer to the prayers that Bud and I have raised to him daily. Despite all the work and anxiety, the interruptions and sacrifices that children demand of us, there really are few greater gifts that God can give to us. Through our children's eyes we see the world in a new light; by them we claim a stake in the future; and from them we receive a small portion of the unmerited love of God. Little children have a marvelous capacity to forgive erring and ignorant parents. They also bestow a love unearned and uncalculated.

Children teach us a lot about ourselves. We find out that maybe we are not so good as we thought, that we can get tired and angry for petty reasons, that we do not know it all, and that we do not have all the ability and wisdom we need satisfactorily to raise a child, much less to run our own lives or to shape our world. Children teach us humility, which is necessary for faith.

But children also teach us that sometimes we are better than we thought—that we can go without sleep to sit up all night with a vomiting child, that we can gladly sacrifice time or material possessions to meet a child's needs, that we can love another unconditionally, even when a child is acting totally unlovably. Raising children is to be schooled in the Christian way of living. And having helped raised two wonderful human beings, I know that they also have helped "raise" me. Truly, the God who has promised to be with me until he has done all that he has purposed for me has continued to fulfill that promise through the lives of our two children.

❖ ❖ ❖ ❖ ❖ ❖

Lancaster and Ecumenism

During our years in Lancaster, Pennsylvania, 1958–1973, I was very much a typical American housewife, getting together with other faculty wives for coffee and desserts and gossip, attending the women's meetings at church, raising the kids, and cleaning and cooking.

We first moved into a seminary-owned, semidetached row house—those dwellings that are so typical of old Pennsylvania towns. They are one room wide, with rooms arranged behind one another in a boxcar fashion, three stories high with a basement beneath, set close to the street with a long narrow backyard behind. A semidetached shares a wall with the neighbor, and Bud was up with a rifle our first night there, looking for the intruder who was climbing our stairs. We soon learned that such noises came from the other side of the common wall.

The adjacent backyards, with only separating fences, afforded wonderful neighborhood community, however, and we neighborhood women spent many hours talking, as we hung up our wash on the clotheslines. Although clothes driers and similar labor-saving devices have spared women a lot of time and work, they have also had the effect of isolating us all in our homes.

Lancaster had excellent public schools, and the children flourished in that old-town, settled environment.

Indeed, so rooted was the community that you could buy cheap auto insurance that was valid only if you limited your driving to Lancaster County.

But roots and tradition are good for children, and we never had any crisis with them. To be sure, Mark accidentally threw a baseball through the living room window once, and in the seventh grade had a habit of losing his schoolbooks. But we came to learn that children do pretty much what their parents expect of them. Many parents have remarked that they dread their children's teenage years and expect the youth to go wild. If that is the expectation, the children will oblige. But if you expect them to be decent, responsible citizens, they will fulfill that expectation also.

I sometimes think that the crucial characteristic of loving and disciplining parenthood is an intense, consistent interest in what our children are becoming. I know when my own parents died in 1973 and 1974, I realized that I had lost the two persons in my world who cared desperately what was happening to me and what sort of person I was becoming. That is an attitude that gets communicated to our offspring, and it was an attitude that our parents passed on to Bud and me.

When Marie was in kindergarten, we decided to buy our own home one block up the street. Marie informed her teacher on a Friday that we were moving, whereupon the teacher gathered together all of Marie's papers, gave her the treats that would be given out at a future party, and told her goodbye. The next Monday Marie showed up in school. "I thought you were moving," puzzled the teacher. "We did," piped Marie. Such are the ways of little children that add laughter to our lives.

Besides being a housewife in Lancaster, I also began my teaching career at the United Church of Christ seminary there. Both Bud and I were members of that denomination. Bud's father was originally a pastor in the Evangelical and Reformed Church, and Bud had his membership there. When we were married, I therefore transferred my Presbyterian membership to the E and R Church so that we would belong together. Subsequently, the Evangelical and Reformed Church merged with the Congregational Christian Churches to form the United Church of Christ. In fact, I was ordained in 1975 in that communion. But when the E and R denomination lost its Reformed polity in its merger with the CC Church, and after it became "politically correct" by dropping its confession of Jesus as Lord—the earliest confession of the New Testament churches—we transferred our ordinations to the Presbyterian Church (U.S.A.). We are Reformed in our bones, emphasizing the sovereignty of God and the authority of the Word, and I for one could not stomach the UCC's avoidance of the lordship of Christ.

In the beginning, I taught only Old Testament theology at Lancaster Seminary. In that capacity, I served as a visiting professor at Gettysburg and Pittsburgh seminaries, driving or flying to those locations for one day's classes every week for one term. Soon, however, I was also asked to give Old Testament seminars at Lancaster, dealing with various portions of the Old Testament.

Because I had studied with von Rad in Heidelberg and had read the two volumes of his *Old Testament Theology,* I adopted his methodology of dividing the Old Testament into three Heilsgeschichte (salvation history) units, each with its own major theological testimony—the theology of the Hexateuch, Davidic royal theology, and the theology of the prophets, with the Writings forming the response to the three. Though each theological collection is intimately related to the others and though each contains many different voices, that scheme has enabled me to organize the vast amount of material found in the Old Testament in a workable and teachable fashion.

The more I worked with the texts, the more I became convinced that Israel's witness in the Old Testament centers around the promises of God and his working in the fulfillment of those promises. At three decisive moments in Israel's life, God breaks into human history and utters his Word, and the whole story of the Bible, then, in both Old Testament and New, concerns God's action to fulfill those words.

Specifically, God gives to Abraham a fourfold promise. He promises to give Abraham's descendants a land to call their own, to make them a great nation, to enter into covenant with them, and to bring blessing on all the families of the earth through them. The prelude to that promise is the primeval history in Genesis 1–11, in which human beings have lost their land of paradise; they have been set under the judgment that has brought broken community, ruined earth, and death; they have lost their relation with God and know only a cursed existence. God therefore sets out through Abraham and his descendants to turn that curse into blessing and to restore the goodness of his creation that he intended in the beginning for all peoples everywhere. Added to that promise to Abraham, then, in the tenth century B.C., is the promise to David that there will never be lacking a Davidic heir to sit upon the throne.

By means of God's working through his further revelatory words to the prophets of the Old Testament, those promises are carried forward. But Israel is shown to be faithless to her God-given role to be God's covenant partner and to be the medium of God's blessing on all the families of the earth. Through the pronouncements of the preexilic prophets, therefore, God works to bring about the destruction of Israel's northern kingdom and to send the people of the southern kingdom into Babylonian exile. It seems as if God has taken back all of his promises. Israel loses her land, her population is greatly reduced and her nationhood lost, her Davidic king is taken into exile, and instead of being a source of blessing in the earth, Israel becomes a source of hissing and curse: "May you be cursed as Israel is cursed."

Yet, even in the midst of ruin and exile, the prophets announce that the Word of God stands forever and that the Lord will redeem Israel by a new act of salvation that will at the same time fulfill all of his past promises to his chosen people. In the fullness of time, therefore, God sends his only begotten Son—a descendant of David and of Abraham—in whom, writes Paul, all the promises of God find their "yes" (2 Cor. 1:20). Christ, the Davidic Messiah, becomes the cornerstone of God's new covenant people, the source of blessing for all peoples everywhere, and the Shepherd who leads his flock toward their promised place of rest in his kingdom-land. At the same time, the promise is renewed that all Israel of the Mosaic covenant in the future will be saved (Rom. 11:26).

From those insights, here briefly outlined, the scriptures became a unified story for me, and initially they resulted in my first book in 1962, *The Old Testament Roots of Our Faith* (New York and Nashville: Abingdon Press), to which Bud then added his contributions and shared in the authorship. The book has been reissued several times by three different publishers and is still in print. But in lectures throughout the nation I have also presented the story and the details of that saving history to hundreds of church members.

When God's activity in human life is understood as his work to fulfill his concrete promises given us in the scriptures, God is no longer understood as Being, à la Tillich, or as static Presence to be discovered by us, as he is so often popularly conceived. Rather, God is active Creator and Lord, who is working out his purpose and who has revealed to us that he is engaged in every relationship and circumstance of human and natural life. Moreover, that purpose concerns not only the biblical past, but is seen to be the ongoing divine activity in which we in the present, and all in the past and future, are included. A historical stream of God's saving work unites past, present, and future, and our lives have worth and meaning as they accord with that ongoing work of our Lord.

Our time at Lancaster was interrupted for a few months. In 1963, Bud was granted a sabbatical leave from the seminary to teach for four months at the Ecumenical Institute in Bossey, near Geneva, Switzerland, and we were granted the privilege of living there for eight. We packed up children and belongings and set out on another adventure.

Bossey was a beautiful site, located in the Swiss countryside, with cows grazing and clanging their bells in the meadows, and the Institute's chateau and other buildings facing the snow-covered Alps. We were housed in an old farmhouse, adjacent to a barn, about a quarter of a mile down the road from the chateau. It was a scene straight out of *Heidi*. But it was also somewhat primitive. I washed clothes by hand in the bathtub. The house was dreadfully cold in the winter. And every night we heard the rats scratching and scurrying between the walls and over the ceiling. We ate most of our meals at the chateau and accustomed ourselves to dishes like onion pie or cream of wheat with tomato sauce, although occasionally we had eggs or delicious venison. Nevertheless, those eight months were a remarkable treat.

Theological students and pastors came to the school from forty different foreign countries for the four months' course, whose topic that year was "Syncretism." We became good friends with Christians from Africa, New Zealand, Britain, the Netherlands, Switzerland, Germany, Scandinavia, Japan, Brazil, and Yugoslavia. An accomplished theological student from the Netherlands gave Mark piano lessons. The first black Methodist bishop from Sierra Leone told us about worship in his country. A black student from South Africa filled us in on apartheid. A Japanese and a New Zealander came to Marie's fifth birthday party. It was an international gathering of Christians from around the world. Not only we but also our children experienced in worship and study the abiding fellowship of the one holy catholic church. We have kept up our correspondence with some of those students through the years, and our special friend, the German dietitian, whom the children called Tanta (Aunt) Inge, has visited us twice in this country. She told us later that when we Americans first arrived at Bossey, she hated us. Her father had died from exposure, patrolling the North Sea in the Nazi navy, and she had suffered starvation after the defeat of Hitler's Germany. But the gospel of Jesus Christ overcomes past enmities, and our common Lord binds his faithful followers together in a relationship transcending all boundaries.

While Bud was busy with his lectures for the students, I taught Mark from his third grade books. We accomplished in two hours every morning what it took his classmates at home several days to master. He was a whiz in math and spelling when he got home, but I overlooked his instruction in penmanship, fortunately now an insignificant deficit in this age of computers.

One can look at scenery only so long, so despite the fact that we did a lot of touring through Switzerland in a borrowed car, I had nothing else that I particularly had to do. Because they had no other playmates, the children occupied themselves with play together, and they formed a friendship that both of them still cherish. But to fill up my time, I wrote a book entitled *The Feminine Crisis in Christian Faith* (New York and Nashville: Abingdon Press) that was published in 1965. It drew on my experiences of the religion that I had observed among church women at home, many of whom were simply immersed in a worship of a God of nature and almost totally ignorant of biblical understandings. In a way, the book was a prelude to my critique of the modern radical feminist movement that has identified God with the vital forces in nature and has reimagined him as a sort of great world soul that inhabits all things and persons. The loss of the transcendence of the biblical God or the blurring of the line between God's transcendence and his immanence has been and still is the basic distortion characteristic of radical feminists' religious writings—a distortion that has led them astray. But the overwhelming holiness and awe-inspiring mystery and power of that transcendence are revealed only through the scriptures. Sadly, the radical feminists have rejected the scriptures as "patriarchal" documents and have drowned out the Word of God with their own preconceived views and strident claims to be "victims."

One of the reasons that the radical feminists' views have found some ready audiences is that so few people have an understanding of the biblical view of God's relation to the natural world. The church in our time has preserved a fully developed doctrine of redemption, but it has neglected the doctrine of creation. I later made an attempt to compensate for that neglect when I was invited to give the Payton Lectures at Fuller Theological Seminary. I lectured on "Nature, God, and Pulpit," later incorporating the lectures in a book with the same title (Grand Rapids: Wm. B. Eerdmans Publishing Co., 1992). The book discusses all of the biblical material concerned with God's relation to the created world, while at the same time giving some attention to the correlation of the Bible's views with modern science.

One evening as we sat reading in our farmhouse in Bossey, a German student knocked at our door. "Kennedy ist geschossen worden" (Kennedy has been shot), he told us. For several days, we and the other Americans at the school stayed glued to the Armed Forces radio, trying to imagine what our country was going through. It was an especially agonizing time for one of the women from Dallas, Texas, made more terrible still after Oswald himself was shot. Some of the Swiss vowed that Oswald was part of a plot to overthrow the government. We assured them that the U.S. government was firmly intact, but it was very difficult to be out of the States in the midst of such a crisis.

Like so many seminaries in this country in recent years, Lancaster experienced a loss of faculty and change of administration at the end of the 60s that boded ill for its future direction, especially because it was wed to a denomination that had renounced, or at least was avoiding, the lordship of Christ. In 1973, Bud accepted the call to be a professor of New Testament at Union Theological Seminary in Richmond, Virginia, a seminary of the Presbyterian Church U.S. Once again, a kindly God was directing our paths.

That same God had used a trivial event to set Bud on his scholarly work, however. When Mark entered public high school in Lancaster, Bud had to get up every morning at 6:00 A.M. to drive Mark to school on time. Suddenly my husband had all sorts of morning time on his hands. He had already written his book *An Introduction to the New Hermeneutic* (Philadelphia: Westminster Press, 1969), but now he began to do serious work on the Gospel of Mark, uncovering the miracle catenae in that book. That led to Bud's leadership in the Society of Biblical Literature and recognition in the scholarly world. Since that time Bud has been president of both the SBL and the Catholic Biblical Association—the only Protestant ever so named—as well as the author of many books and articles, the General Editor of *Harper's Bible Dictionary*, General Editor of New Testament books in the Interpretation commentary series, and Editor of the periodical *Interpretation*. God, it seems, presents us with opportunities to further his gospel if we are willing to serve and work.

Teaching and Preaching

The year 1973 was a time of momentous change in our lives. We bought a house in Richmond, Virginia, said goodbye to our friends in Lancaster, and moved to our new home in July. Mother died in August. Mark left for college at Harvard in September. Marie entered high school, and we began our teaching at Union Theological Seminary. All the changes could have overwhelmed us, but we were welcomed so warmly into the Union Seminary community, and we were so glad to be there, that we quickly adjusted.

Marie, however, suffered the trauma that we were spared. We had always supported public education and were firm believers in the integration of the public schools, so Marie willingly began her ninth grade at the public John Marshall High School. Some of Union's faculty had been among those fighting to integrate schools in the South, and a few assured us that students could get a good education at John Marshall. Sadly, the opposite turned out to be the case.

The student body and faculty at John Marshall were about 85 percent African American, which did not bother us in the least. After all, I was raised by a mother who had been fighting for civil rights all of her life, and our children had learned to be friends with those of every race both in their previous schooling and during our months at

Bossey. So Marie gave it her all, even considering running for class president. Her initial enthusiasm was quickly dampened, however.

Because Marie was an excellent student, she was placed in the supposed "Honors track." But the English reading in that track was *Jonathan Livingston Seagull.* Marie was asked to write innumerable term papers, which were returned with a grade of A+ but with no further comment on them. One of her classmates even made up term papers containing fictional information and foot-notes and received the same high grade. One social stud-ies teacher insisted that Mt. Everest was in Alaska and, when confronted with evidence on a map, tried to cover her mistake by claiming, "That's an old map." French class was dominated by discipline problems. Marie lost a year of French and math. Once, when she went to the rest room, she found students pulling out and scattering paper towels throughout the bathroom. She did not dare to say a word, however, for fear of bodily harm, a fate that had met some other students at the school. In a talk with the guidance counselor of the school, Marie was told that she should plan to be a beautician. She simply looked at the counselor and left.

By Christmastime, our daughter was thoroughly de-pressed and physically sick. She had always loved school, but it had become for her a place without reward, without learning, without joy. We were alarmed by her depression and even suicidal thoughts, so we enrolled her for the next year in the fine private Collegiate School in Richmond. The thought that she would be able to leave John Marshall High School sustained her for the next months.

Like most private places of learning, Collegiate's stu-dent body was a homogenous group of middle- and upper-class students. All of us regretted the loss of a mixed community of learning, because both of the children had profited from such a mixture in Lancaster. Equally, we grieved for the African American parents who could not afford to send their children to private schools. But we were unwilling to risk our daughter's future and, literally, her life for the sake of our views. Once she made up her loss of French and math instruction, Marie graduated as the valedictorian of her class at Collegiate and went on to successful education at Brown University and the University of Virginia's law school.

It is questionable if Richmond's schools have improved very much. Because of Marie's experience, I am a firm supporter of charter schools and of school vouchers, both of which unfortunately have been opposed by the National Education Association. The result is that we are destroying the lives of thousands of African American students, who are receiving at best a very inferior education. It is no wonder that so many are unable to find employment.

When we began our teaching at Union Seminary, it was a bastion of male dominance. The famed educator Sara Little taught religious education as an adjunct professor from the Presbyterian School of Christian Education across the street. Otherwise, all on the faculty were male. Indeed, it was an unwritten policy that wives of faculty members could not even fill secretarial positions; the seminary wanted no complications in hiring and firing. So what to do with me?

The seminary solved the problem by appointing me as a visiting and, later, adjunct professor, a somewhat ambiguous title, because I often taught a full load of courses and, for one term, when Wellford Hobbie succumbed to cancer, was the sole professor in homiletics. After employing me for some years, the seminary opened its doors to women professors and to the calling of married couples to teach.

When we arrived at Union, it certainly did not need anyone to teach Old Testament. John Bright, James Mays, and Patrick Miller all were in that department. But there was an opening in homiletics. By the mysterious guiding of God, I had just written a book entitled *The Old Testament and the Proclamation of the Gospel* (Philadelphia: Westminster Press, 1973), a volume that grew out of my conviction that unless the study of the Old Testament issues in preaching, the Book of the Old Covenant hasn't been properly understood. The seminary therefore asked me to become a visiting professor in homiletics, a switch in my field that I welcomed. Though I have occasionally substituted for a professor on sabbatical in the Old Testament department, and though I have written a number of Old Testament commentaries and articles, most of my books and seminary teaching has been concerned with preaching.

I had no Ph.D. in homiletics, as do so many homiletics professors now. I therefore had to draw on my own rather extensive preaching experience to teach that discipline. I had studied homiletics as a seminary student with Paul Scherer and George Buttrick, both of whom were outstanding preachers in the past generation. Buttrick had furnished me with some practical guides; Scherer had inspired me with the possibility of art and beauty in a sermon. But for the most part, the homiletical guides that I followed came from meditating on what had been effective in my own sermons in the past.

I quickly learned, however, that my doctorate in the biblical field gave me a distinct advantage in homiletics, for I was trained to concentrate on the biblical text and to uncover its message. Only out of that basis, then, could a sermon be developed. The basic fault of all poor sermons is their ignorance of the biblical text or their inability to hear that text speaking to the present congregation. But from the time of my study with Muilenburg, on throughout my career, the biblical texts have been for me the source of the speaking of the living, present God. My efforts in teaching were to communicate that orientation to my students. If Union students learned nothing else, they learned they had to preach from the scriptures, a distinction that divides them from many of the churches' preachers.

One of the joys of teaching homiletics is that the professor is able to see very clearly evidence of students' progress. When my students first began their instruction in preaching, few of them had ever spoken before in front of a group. Most of them were nervous during their first try. In fact, I had one student whose mouth became so dry that he had to stop and get a drink of water before he could move his tongue. But along with overcoming their fright, the students had to master multiple tasks—how to stand, move, handle notes or a manuscript, project their voices, vary their delivery, maintain eye contact with the congregation, react to congregational feedback—those dozens of homiletical techniques that go into effective preaching. Few congregations realize what is involved in delivering a sermon and how important those techniques are for making or breaking a sermon.

Students also had to learn to get a sermon form under their belts. No matter what type of sermon a preacher adopts—narrative, expository, topical, and so forth— sermons are an art form unto themselves. They are not essays, entertainment, topical discussions, philosophical musings, prophetic disquisitions. They are the direct conversation of God with his gathered people. They have beginnings and closures, emphases and climaxes, movement and logical unity—the whole gathered around a principal theme. And students have to learn to let the biblical text shape their thought into that unique and artistic form.

Most important, students must learn to marshal all of their theological, biblical, historical, and pastoral training—for preaching is the queen of the theological disciplines—in order to set forth the Word of God from the biblical text in such a manner that it engages not only the minds but also the hearts and experiences of their listeners.

The only way students learn to do all of those things, however, is by practicing them, writing and delivering sermons, and then having their products critiqued by classmates and professor. Students cannot learn to preach just by hearing lectures about preaching. They have to try it themselves, over and over again, each time learning a little more, until they become competent enough to be let loose on the church.

As my students practiced and learned, I had the joy of watching them grow in the mastery of their craft until the difference between their inept beginnings and their final preaching in class was like the difference between night and day. That is a joy not so evidently given to seminary professors in other disciplines. Who knows what a student has actually absorbed in theology class or church history, other than what is written on the final exam? But homiletics professors know, because they see and hear it in the student's actual preaching.

In addition to teaching homiletics, I also began offering at Union an elective course in a survey of the English Bible and its various theologies. That meant that I had to join Old Testament theology and New, a requirement that sent me to further reading in the New Testament field. It was, however, a welcomed extension of my learning, because I had long been convinced that the two testaments were joined in one ongoing story of God's salvation. Indeed, in *The Old Testament and the Proclamation of the Gospel* I had already pointed out that the testimony to Jesus Christ in the New Testament is based primarily on theologies and figures drawn from the Old Testament. Jesus is, in the New Testament witness, the promised Davidic Messiah, the begotten Son of God as Israel was the adopted son, the good Shepherd of Ezekiel 34, the Suffering Servant of Second Isaiah, the prophetic intercessor, and the high priest after the order of Melchizedek. Exodus, Sinai, Levitical, and Psalm traditions are all used to portray his death. The full Word of the Old Testament is incarnated in his birth. The promises of the Old Testament partly interpret his resurrection. It is clear that Jesus Christ cannot be understood apart from Israel's testimony.

Similarly, I had long recognized that the church's life parallels that of Israel, as was promised in the new age by the prophets. Both Israel and the church are redeemed out of slavery, long before they deserve it. Both are made God's elected people, his kingdom of priests and holy nation. Both of them are brought to the table of covenant and promise to serve God alone. Both are always accompanied by God on their journey toward a promised place of rest. Both offer sacrifices of praise to the Lord and are his witnesses to the world. The church cannot know who it is as the "Israel of God" (Gal. 6:16) apart from the Old Testament. Thus, a joining of Old Testament and New in my survey course was a welcomed extension of my teaching that accorded completely with my own study of the scriptures.

Students came to call that survey course "Betty's Bible Blitz"—a title that I enjoyed—because it initially was given during the one-month January term, when the students took only that single course. They were required to read through the entire Bible and to pass detailed quizzes on its content in preparation for their ordination exams, while I devoted the lectures to biblical theology. The course was intense and demanding, but it was usually filled with dozens of students who devoured the theology but who also outscored all other Presbyterian seminary students on their ordination Bible content exam.

In addition to teaching at the seminary, I was enlisted by Union during my first ten years on the campus to teach satellite courses for pastors pursuing their D.Min. degrees out in the field. Small groups of pastors would gather at Norfolk, Charleston, West Virginia, Charlotte, or Raleigh, and I would fly in for one day's instruction per week in the ten-week term. It was a wonderful way to be introduced to the southern branch of the Presbyterian Church and to get to know pastors throughout the Virginias and North Carolina.

At the same time, Duke Divinity School in Durham, North Carolina, asked me to teach homiletics for them one day per week for one term. I spent a lot of time on airplanes, but I also gained insight into the type of preaching that was being carried on in various churches, which in turn helped me in shaping the instruction that I was giving on Union's campus. The most frequent mistakes in sermon preparation became clear to me: sermon introductions that are too long or that start the congregation thinking about a subject unrelated to what follows in the rest of the sermon; long illustrations and quotations that interrupt the flow of the sermon; conclusions that suddenly introduce a new thought or scripture verse. Out of that experience, I was able to formulate standard guides for sermon construction, some of which are now set forth in the little book I wrote for Pulpit Nominating Committees, *So You're Looking for a New Preacher* (Grand Rapids: Wm. B. Eerdmans Publishing Co., 1991).

While teaching at Duke, I had a valuable experience with one student that has remained with me ever since. There was in my class a young man who was on the verge of giving up all thought of entering the preaching ministry. He had been in homiletics classes in which his professor insisted that he preach from memory, without a manuscript in front of him in the pulpit. He had been totally unable to do so, but he was going to give it one more try. When I discovered his plight, I told him, "For goodness sakes, take whatever you want into the pulpit—a full manuscript, an outline, notes, whatever you feel most comfortable with. Just don't read a manuscript. Go over it often enough ahead of time so it is your natural way of speaking." The student retrieved his manuscript, and from his mouth emerged a powerful and beautiful sermon in language honed and shaped to its full power—language that he could not marshal from memory but was there if he could glance at it occasionally. A strict, legalistic rule about sermon delivery had almost destroyed his ministry. Set free from the law, his words flowed forth.

That student was unusual, however, in his ability to handle language. Actually, we have very few ministers who are rhetoricians and who can use the full power and beauty of the English language in their preaching. Few are cognizant of the rhythm of English; few know where to use exactly the right word to maintain that rhythm or to break it for emphasis. Few know how to make words into pictures that implant themselves in a congregation's mind.

I suppose one of the reasons for that lack is that we moderns are not used to words; instead, we rely on the visual, an outgrowth of our exposure to television. But the biblical faith is a "hearing faith": "Hear, O Israel!" "Thus says the Lord!" "What is this you have done?" "Answer me!" It has even been suggested that part of the reason for the ethical breakdown in our society is that we no longer know how to hear.

Certainly part of our deficiency is also due to our neglect of reading in great literature. I think I first learned the rhythm of the English language from the book that has been called "the noblest monument of English prose," the King James Bible. I would not want us to return to that translation, but certainly some of our modern translations of the scriptures are a far cry from that monument. Actually, they do not even capture the force of the original biblical Hebrew or Greek. Powerful poetry and prose are found in the scriptures; unfortunately, we have lost some of that power in some translations.

Similarly, by our neglect of the great traditional prayers of the church we have impoverished our language. The collects in the *Book of Common Prayer* are polished masterpieces that show many of our modern prayers to God to be thoughtless and demeaning recitations addressed not really to God but to the bowed congregation. But we have a glorious God who has offered us glorious gifts of love. I have always thought that our language in prayers and sermons should bear some hint of that glory, some reflection of the boundless treasures from the riches of Jesus Christ.

As a result, I taught a course at Union Seminary that had the title "The Language of the Sermon." Most of the reading in the course, to mention only part of it, was done in good contemporary literature—in the plays of Christopher Fry, T. S. Eliot, Robert Bolt, G. B. Shaw; in the books of Annie Dillard, Loren Eiseley, Lewis Thomas; in the sermons of James S. Stewart, Paul Scherer, Edmund Steimle; in the poetry of Emily Dickinson, W. H. Auden, Gerard Manley Hopkins, Amos Wilder. In addition, there were assigned books about writing from Strunk and White, Katherine Paterson, and Eudora Welty. All were intended as an effort to teach the students what good English sounds like, to stimulate their minds and imaginations, and to broaden their vocabularies and illustrative powers.

I also wrote a book entitled *Creative Preaching: Finding the Words,* in which I wrote these words:

> A preacher's tools are words, shaped into the rhythms and cadences, the fortissimos and whispers, the conversation and confrontation of oral speech. To neglect the mastery of words is to be like a carpenter who throws away his saw and sets out to fashion a piece of fine furniture, using nothing but an ax. We may hack away at a congregation with tools totally inappropriate to their purpose—dull words, misleading sentences, repetitious paragraphs, ineffective illustrations. Or we may take up the fine tool of language, honed and polished to a cutting edge, and then trust that God will use it to fashion his people—his "work of art in Christ" (Eph. 2:10). The committed preachers—the faithful servants of God—do not neglect their tools! *(Nashville: Abingdon Press, 1980, p. 22)*

I have heard over the years that some of my students have continued their habit of good reading, started first in the classroom, and that it has improved their rhetoric as a result. Reinhold Niebuhr once remarked that he did not like "pretty sermons." To be sure, rhetoric for rhetoric's sake does nothing to advance the gospel. But rhetoric for the sake of the glory of God is a service rendered up to him.

Preaching finally has a sacramental character. That is, it is an action of God toward a gathered congregation. Through the human words of the preacher, taken from the scriptures and illumined by the Holy Spirit, the Word of God written becomes the Word of God spoken. The preacher is the meeting point of those two Words, and when God so wills by his Spirit, the congregation is addressed by their living Lord. For that reason, preaching has the character of direct address. It is not a disquisition *about* God. It is not an objective standing back and discussing a text. It is not human opinion about a religious subject. Preaching is one of the two media the Lord has chosen to act upon his people—the other being the sacraments. "Faith comes from what is heard, and what is heard comes by the preaching of Christ" (Rom. 10:17). Through preaching our words become God's Word; God judges, redeems, transforms, sanctifies the lives of his beloved people. I can imagine no higher or more humbling calling.

Sex and the Church

When our daughter Marie left for college in 1977, she was prepared and eager to begin to make her way on her own, so she had no difficulty adjusting to life away from home. Rather, her major problem was dealing with a roommate who insisted on having her boyfriend sleep with her every weekend. Marie had no desire to remain in the room with the fornicating couple, and she continually lost sleep looking for some place else to put her sleeping bag. Another girl in the dorm remarked, "That's just something you have to get used to in college." When Marie sought out the college chaplain for counsel, he told her, "Don't worry about it." Marie did worry about it, however, and soon found herself another roommate. But it brought home to me, in a very personal way, the promiscuous situation on most of our college campuses and the widespread acceptance in our culture of such wide-open sex.

Ours is a whoring society in which almost any sexual relation is acceptable. National leaders are forgiven their extramarital affairs. Admired television and movie stars have children out of wedlock and have no intention of getting married. Schools hand out condoms, because they presuppose that students will be sexually active. And the media drown us in a sea of sex without consequences.

But of course there are consequences. "God is not mocked" (Gal. 6:7), and we are paying the price in widespread venereal disease, the growth of a vast underclass of unwed and poverty-stricken mothers, broken homes and children deprived of parents, and a virtual epidemic of abortions that are fostered by our Supreme Court and government.

One of the deplorable aspects of it all has been the attitude of the mainline churches, who have been engulfed by their acquiescence to society's immorality. In 1991, the Presbyterian Church (U.S.A.) issued a Human Sexuality Report that sanctioned any sexual relationship, providing it was carried on in something called "justice-love." Though that report was voted down by a large majority of the church's presbyteries, similar views were recommended again in 1998 in a proposed amendment to the Presbyterian constitution. Fortunately, those views too were rejected, but the fact that they could be proposed at all is indicative of the state of the Presbyterian Church (U.S.A.).

The scene is little different in most denominations, and it signals a substitution of the authority of the individual for the authority of the Word of God. The Bible is quite clear about God's intentions for sexual behavior. Sexual intercourse is a good and joyous gift of God, given to be used only within the bounds of matrimony, as the final unifying act of a wife and her husband. Further, that gift and its uses are protected in the Bible by the commandments of God in the Old Testament and the teachings of Jesus and the apostles in the New. Jesus teaches that God, in his creation of humankind, made male and female, that the two might become one in matrimony, in the joyous union of one flesh, a union sanctioned by God that no human being is to "put asunder" (Mark 10:6–9).

But swept away by a deconstructionist emphasis on any truth as relative to an individual's opinion, churches have lost their nerve about saying anything that contradicts the ways of an immoral society. As a result, they have lost their distinctive Christian voice and any possibility of exerting influence on the general populace. The loss of that possibility has done nothing but encourage the widespread sexual promiscuity that is now so evident in our high schools, on our college campuses, and in our society at large.

I think I became even more aware of that situation when, in 1988, I was asked by Presbyterians Pro-Life to be their representative on a task force that the PC(USA) General Assembly had mandated to study the issue of abortion after it had heard a powerful talk by Mother Teresa of India. Like most persons in the church, I had given very little thought to the issue of abortion. After all, it hadn't touched my personal life.

I therefore took some time off during the summer before the task force met and studied the scriptures to find out what they had to say about abortion. My church has declared through the ages that the scriptures are our one authority for faith and practice. It seemed to me, therefore, that the Bible was to be the basis of any decisions about abortion or any other current social problem.

I found in my study that there was no specific text in the Bible dealing with abortion other than the disputed text of Exodus 21:22–24. But I also found that there were multiple texts dealing with God's relation to the child in the womb. The Bible clearly states that all of us are created by God, "knit together with bones and sinews" (Job 10:11) in our mothers' wombs. They clearly state that all of us, born and unborn, belong to God and not to ourselves (Pss. 24:1; 95:7; 1 Cor. 10:26, et al.), and that therefore we are not free to do what we like with God's children. I had long known from the Bible that God had a plan that he was working out in my life, so I also knew that God had a plan for each child that he created and that human beings were not to disrupt that plan by aborting their children. The scriptures told me that all of us are created to praise and serve God, but it followed that an aborted child enters only the silence of death. And above all, I read over and over in the scriptures that God wills not death for us, but life, a fact finding its final confirmation in the resurrection of Jesus Christ.

When I began work with the task force I knew therefore that we were dealing with the very heart of the Christian faith—with the relation of every human being, born or unborn, to God. That to me was a subject of utmost importance.

As I worked on that task force, I was overwhelmed by the statistics that characterize our society. I learned that one and one-half million children every year are being forcefully removed from their mothers' wombs and consigned to medical waste buckets. Adding up the total of children lost since the passage of *Roe vs. Wade* in 1973, that amounts to more human beings killed than in all our wars. But according to surveys conducted by the Alan Gutmacher Institute, the majority of those obtaining abortions are not the poor, as I had believed, but white women under the age of twenty-five, who have never been married and who have never before had a child—in short, those who have engaged in extramarital sex. I found out that their abortions do not solve the problems of those women, however. Rather, the majority of them later suffer postabortion psychological trauma, sometimes for years after the operation. I learned that the largest abortion provider in the United States is the Planned Parenthood Society, which is doing very little to foster adoption. I found that few churches are even discussing the issue, much less offering help to women with problem pregnancies. The attitude of the churches, and especially of the "tall steeple" churches, is that they do not want to cause dissension in their congregations. Yet I also read that the majority of women who have abortions state that they would never have gone through the procedure had they known someone who would help them.

Probably the thing that later shocked me most, however, was a statement, published in the newspaper, quoting the newly elected president of the Planned Parenthood Society of America. "Abortion is where the rubber hits the road," she said, "the line in the sand for women to become fully equal citizens" (*Richmond Times-Dispatch*, Dec. 13, 1992). In other words, she believed that women could have the same sexual freedom as men, and that if a pregnancy resulted, they could just have an abortion. Women could be free by killing their children—a view still held by many radical feminists!

I knew, however, where my freedom and equality lay—in Jesus Christ, who has overcome the battle of the sexes and who has made us all one in him, male and female, Jew and Gentile, slave and free (Gal. 3:28).

The majority of clergy and laity on the PC(USA) task force did not start with God's Word in the scriptures, however. They started with human problems. In their 1992 report to the General Assembly, entitled "Problem Pregnancies and Abortion," they ended up asserting, first, that the child in the womb might not yet be human, a statement contrary to the scriptures and most genetic textbooks.

Second, they stated that though they hoped the number of abortions could be lessened, there nevertheless were situations, even beyond instances of rape, incest, or threat to the mother's life, in which abortion was morally permissible. A few of us wrote a minority report to the contrary, but it was rejected by the vote of the General Assembly.

The majority paper did state that there were differing views on the issue and that the church should therefore allow, in its publications and statements, room for other views. The PC(USA) has not, however, given that room. Instead, the denomination continues to give financial support to organizations within the church that advocate abortion, such as PARO (Presbyterians Affirming Reproductive Options), but they give no funds to pro-life groups. They refuse to publish any pro-life materials, and their health plan continues to pay for any abortion obtained by female clergy or spouses of male clergy, with no questions asked about the reason for the abortion. Through consistent lobbying, however, Presbyterians Pro-Life has persuaded the pension board in charge of the health plan to allow churches who conscientiously object to abortion to set aside, in a separate fund, their money paid into the obligatory plan.

After my work on the task force, I joined the national board of Presbyterians Pro-Life and have written numerous articles and given some talks before church groups on the subject. In 1995, Terry Schlossberg, the executive director of PPL, and I coauthored a book entitled *Not My Own: Abortion and the Marks of the Church* (Grand Rapids: Wm. B. Eerdmans Publishing Co.). Co-authoring was a daunting task, because we worked at different speeds over three years of discussion and writing. In the book we attempt to set the whole problem of abortion, not in a legal and legislative context, but squarely in the framework of the preaching and sacraments ("the marks") of the church. Abortion finally is a moral problem having to do with our relation to God, and only in the context of that relation will the problem of abortion—and of sexuality—be solved.

It is difficult in the church to take a biblical stance on any social issue, because our society and our churches are so divided into separate ideological groups and caucuses that one immediately becomes labeled as a one-issue person if one takes a position. Spokespersons for an issue are then judged to be conservative, moderate, or liberal on the basis of their advocacy. Despite my work in Presbyterians Pro-Life, I have largely avoided such labeling in most places, however, by continuing to write and speak on the other subjects of biblical study, preaching, and occasionally marriage and family. Nor has my teaching, preaching, and writing been limited to the Presbyterian Church. I have been given the opportunity to preach in hundreds of churches of many different denominations, to speak on college campuses across the nation, and to address conferences and seminary students in many different communions. It has given me the opportunity to observe the life of the one Body of Christ, irrespective of denominational ties. The church of Jesus Christ is in fact one church, no matter how we may label ourselves, confessing "one Lord, one faith, one baptism, one God and Father of us all" (Eph. 4:5–6). Our major struggle these days, however, is to be the church, founded on the Word of God, and not a body absorbed into the ways of our sinful culture.

Discipline for the Journey

All during my professional career I have written books and articles, a task that I thoroughly enjoy. But when you write for the public, various groups then ask you to speak. There are hundreds of opportunities. Churches often want guest preachers or teachers, and one of the satisfying aspects of my visits to some of those churches has been to see my former students at work in their ministries. It is encouraging, and yet also humbling, to realize that I have had a hand in training that man or woman who is now so capably filling a pulpit or leading in worship.

Some churches have regular endowed lectureships, as do many seminaries of different denominations, both in this country and in Canada. There are literally hundreds of conferences that take place throughout the country for which one is sometimes invited to lecture. Colleges and universities, large and small, have asked me to preach or to give the Staley Foundation's nationally endowed lectures, very often on the subject of "Having a Christian Marriage in Our Society."

It is always interesting to hear how I am introduced before I speak to a group. Unless you know German, the name "Achtemeier" is not easy to pronounce, much less spell, and the name has been subject to all sorts of variations—"Achteheimer," "Okmeyer," "Okheimer." At one church where I was to preach, a female session member was invited by the pastor to pray with us before the service. Laying her hand on my head, she prayed, "And O Lord, bless Dr. Oppenheimer." Bud and I later agreed that Oppenheimer probably needed the blessing too!

Perhaps one of my most moving experiences was being asked to be Chaplain of the Week at the Chautauqua Institution in New York, where I had spent so many summers with my mother during my junior high school days. Services there are held in an enormous 10,000 seat amphitheater. As I preached to that crowd, I could vividly recall Mother sitting in her accustomed seat part way up on the left from the podium. It brought forth some private tears from me.

Traveling and speaking can be exhausting. When I first began such work, plane travel was rather enjoyable. But it is no longer what it used to be, and one puts up with the inevitable travel delays, missed connections, and lost luggage. Yet there are hundreds of seminary and university professors and well-known preachers who are engaged in that peripatetic pursuit, jetting hither and yon, with some of them making almost a full-time career of it.

It is exhilarating, to be sure, to be praised, sometimes pampered, housed and fed and paid. And the interaction with church members, college students, and fellow preachers is both instructive and encouraging. Yet one of the terrible temptations of such travel and speaking is to sink into pride and to believe that one is an important promoter of God's kingdom.

Though I continue to travel and speak throughout the United States and Canada, I sometimes wonder if there are any lasting results from such activity. Has anyone in the audience really absorbed any new learning or been prompted to trust God more fully? To be sure, I have sometimes heard expressions of new faith found or a marriage saved or new insights gleaned. But for the most part, I simply have to trust that the Word of God will make its way in human hearts by the work of the Holy Spirit. Any good results of such mission work come from God and not from human efforts.

The other temptation of such a traveling ministry is to let it sink into routine, to automatically deliver a sermon or lecture that one has given several times before in some other place, to cease to care about the faces and faith and welfare of the persons sitting out in the audience or congregation. When this happens, one has become an unworthy steward of the mysteries of God. I think that can only be combatted by remembering that the Christian gospel is a matter of eternal life or death for everyone who hears it, and that one is responsible to the Lord who has accompanied one on the trip and who is present at that moment. It is that remembrance that ultimately motivates my journeys.

I do not think it is possible to carry on a worthy ministry or, indeed, to lead anything approaching a Christian life without the constant support of Christian discipline. Discipline is not a favorite word of people in our society these days, but Christians cannot exist without it. It consists of four absolutely necessary practices: regular corporate worship, consistent day-by-day study of the scriptures, regular private prayer, and constant attempts to be obedient to God.

There have been so many times in my life when I have gone to church, concerned about some problem or thinking about other matters, and then, when I have heard the call to worship, suddenly been lifted out of myself to concentrate instead on God. "The Lord is in his holy temple. Let all the earth keep silence before him." God is present, confronting me. All matters fall into proper perspective. His power, his love, his guidance encompass my thoughts and living, and all other matters become subject to praising and worshiping him for his assuring, all-mighty rule. God becomes all, and I am set free of myself to sing God's glory with my fellow worshippers, to join in their common prayers, to eat and drink with them at our Lord's Table, and to place myself with them under the authority of the Word.

More than that, in the corporate worship of the church I join with all the communion of faithful saints, in heaven and on earth. I become an adopted daughter in the household of faith with Isaiah and with Job, with Luther and with Calvin, with Bonhoeffer and Mother Teresa, and yes, with my faithful loved ones who have died before me. There we are, one great body of faith through the ages, praising the God who has redeemed us in Christ, supporting one another in our trust, and rejoicing in our common heritage. No solitary worship of God can replace the joy of that company, and I, by the grace and guiding of God, have been made a part of it.

I have not learned who God is and what he desires primarily from the liturgy of corporate worship, however. My knowledge of God has come through his Word in the scriptures, and our worship of him is our response to that knowledge. To be sure, the Word is proclaimed in liturgy and sermon in worship, but growth in knowledge of God and absorption of "the whole counsel of God" can be had only by regular study of the Bible. Christians cannot mature in faith unless they engage in that study.

Growth in the Christian faith is an ongoing and gradual process. We find that we learn more and more of God's character and will as we day-by-day read his written Word. Passages that were obscure ten years ago suddenly break into light. Aspects of God's rule that puzzled us become more and more understandable. Our knowledge of God, though never complete, grows deeper and more secure, and we find our trust firmed and broadened and our hope growing ever more certain.

I have no difficulty engaging in daily Bible study, because that is part of my calling as a teacher and preacher. But I know from countless conversations that it is hard for the average lay person. When can they find the time in this frantic and busy world? The only answer is to set aside a specific time every day and to do it, scheduling it as regularly as fixing supper or going to work. If we want to be Christians, we must read the Bible, chapter by chapter, book by book, over and over again, until it becomes as familiar to us as going to bed. Then we must meditate on the words we have read and ask what God is saying to us through them. I have Christian friends who engage in such consistent practice, and consequently they know our God. Is there any better knowledge we can gain in this world of ours?

There are multiple ways for a person to practice a life of prayer. Although I can describe what I do, it is by no means the only way. Prayer for me takes several forms, but if I want to lead anything approaching a Christian life, I cannot neglect it. I discovered when I was teaching satellite courses for pastors for Union Seminary that the ministers who could not preach were individuals who did not know how to pray. Prayer is our daily God-consciousness, our silent speaking to the One who is with us. If we do not preserve that communion, we forget about our Lord.

All through the day I offer little "arrow prayers" to God. If an ambulance goes by on the street, I ask God to take care of the patient in it. If a family member is traveling, I pray God's protection of them. When I return safely home from a speaking trip, I thank God for returning me to loved ones. Even sometimes when I turn on a lamp, I praise God for the miracle of light. Every occasion is an opportunity for "arrow prayers," for recognition of God's abiding presence. After a while, one's whole life is surrounded by that consciousness. It's very difficult to be downcast or surly if one is expressing thanks to God. Gratitude overcomes our sinful concentration on ourselves.

I also reserve time during daily morning walks or every evening when I go to bed for longer prayer to God. That is when I raise up before my Lord all my concerns and the persons for whom I am responsible. I have a difficult time praying for all persons everywhere. It has always seemed significant to me that we are required in the Bible, not to love all people—which is easy—but just to love our neighbor, a care that may be a great deal more difficult to achieve. So I pray for those known to me—for my husband and children and relatives, for my friends and those whom I know are sick or needy, for work at hand, and for future work to come. All my prayers are set within the petition that I may be a faithful servant of God, useful in his purpose of salvation for his world.

Similarly, I never preach or teach anywhere without private prayer beforehand, asking that my words may be used for the furtherance of God's Word. I do not know how any ministry or any Christian life can be carried on without that petition for God, I know, answers prayers in accordance with his will when they are prayed in sincerity and trust.

There is one type of prayer found in the scriptures that most people never use, and that is prayer for the destruction of evil. In the Psalms, the singers often ask God to do away with some form of evil or wrong. The psalmists do not take such destruction into their own hands but rather ask God to accomplish it. I sometimes have the feeling that our easy accommodation to the wrong in our world is due to the fact that we never ask God to put down and destroy sin's evil, including the evil in our own hearts and lives! But that is a legitimate prayer, according to the scriptures.

Finally, all my prayer is prayed through the mediation or in the name of Jesus Christ, for I also know that apart from Christ's forgiveness and redemption of us, we cannot approach a holy God. Only if God sees Christ's righteousness, and not our sins, do we literally have a prayer before him, for as the prophet says of God, "Thou art of purer eyes than to behold evil and canst not look on wrong" (Hab. 1:13). More than that, Christ himself prays for us, as the New Testament teaches us. It is simply overwhelming to me that the risen Christ remembers and prays for me, as I also pray to him.

Certainly the Christian life is incomplete without also the discipline of obedience, for action must accompany worship, knowledge, and prayer or the latter three are futile. God's will is set forth for us in the scriptures in a multitude of commandments and teachings and stories. Having read and learned of those, we are called to obey. Karl Barth once remarked that the saddest fate that could come to any human being would be to come to the end of our life and to realize that we have been utterly useless in the purpose of God—as if the only epitaph on our tombstone could be a zero. If we are to be of any use whatsoever in the purpose of God, therefore, we must obey God's will set forth for us.

It is not easy to lead a Christian life in our society: to cling to God's truth when all about us are declaring that their opinion is the only truth; to forget about self in a society that seeks only to look out for number one; to hold a marriage and home together when easy divorce has become the custom; to insist on justice at a time when pride of wealth and power are our culture's goals; to be willing to forgive when other persons want only what a wrongdoer deserves.

Obedience to God's will, illumined for us in the scriptures, is very much a matter of taking our wills in hand, of getting out of bed every morning and deciding to be God's person, of setting our feet firmly on God's way and not on our own. The Christian life involves decision and will, self-rule subjected humbly to God's righteous will.

Christians who try to follow God's will in our world know that they cannot be good simply by their own power, however, especially when we live in a society where goodness is out of fashion. The wondrous message of the Christian gospel is that God in Christ not only commands us to be and to do the good but also furnishes us the power to be and to do. God in Christ sends us his Spirit to correct and guide and support us, and we come to realize that it is not we who are working, but Christ who is working in us. Thus obedience to God is marked not by self-righteousness, but by humility that knows that apart from Christ we can do nothing that serves God's purpose.

Helping in the task of Christian obedience are the support and prayers of one's Christian friends. In fact, even a criticism by one's enemy or opponent can correct one's thought and behavior. It has been my blessing to know intimately through the years a few people with whom I can share my deepest thoughts and faith, persons whose commitment to God has inspired and strengthened my own, trustworthy souls on whom I can count for help in time of any need.

In one sense, the life of a woman in academia is a lonely calling. There are not many other women who share my theological journey and work. Usually I am more comfortable talking to male scholars and clergy, as well as to my husband, than to other women. But I have one or two close women friends who are also striving and learning in the faith or who are willing to listen to my musings, and they have continually blessed and comforted my life.

Perhaps one of the most remarkable facts about trying to live in obedience to God's will is that obedience strengthens faith. We are taught in the scriptures that God's way leads to abundant life. I have consistently found that when I try to practice forgiving love, patience, kindness, gentleness, and self-control—those gifts that Paul lists as the fruit of the Spirit (Gal. 5:22–23)—they do indeed yield the abundance that Christ has promised. God's Word proves true, so I trust him even more to guide my daily path. Never has the Father failed me; never has Christ left me desolate. As I experience that more and more, my trust in God is enlarged and deepened.

The Christian way of life is no fairy tale; in the power of the Spirit, it can be lived. Countless Christians through the ages have shown us how. The fruit of worship and Bible study, of prayer and obedience to the Word, is a joy, a peace, an unshakable hope that the world cannot give or take away.

Retirement and the Future

Bud and I retired from teaching at Union Theological Seminary at the end of the 1997 school year. We both decided to retire at the same time, because we wanted to be able to continue to share our schedules and activities together. I had been involved in teaching for forty years, Bud for forty-one years. Because Union now has an entirely different agenda from the one to which we dedicated ourselves, it was a propitious time to leave and to let the younger generation have its way. We have, however, continued to make our home in Richmond, because we do not know a more pleasant place to live.

When friends ask us what we are doing in retirement, we tell them that we have retired but we haven't quit. And indeed, our daily activities are very little different from what they were when we were on the faculty. Thanks be to God, we are both in good health, Bud having successfully been healed from an operation for prostate cancer. Though it takes a little longer in our over-seventy years to do what we plan, and though we don't quite have the reserves of energy that we had twenty years ago, we both are continuing to write and to speak throughout the nation.

Our work keeps us mentally alert. We find that unless we are intellectually engaged, we are not satisfied, a condition that I suppose is true of most former professors. Thus, over the past year I have written a book on *Preaching Hard Texts of the Old Testament* (Peabody, Mass.: Hendrickson Publishing Co, 1998); published a book on *Preaching from the Minor Prophets* (Grand Rapids: Wm. B. Eerdmans Publishing Co., 1998); given a paper on the biblical background of aid to victims of crime; led a seminar for Methodist pastors on biblical authority; written on Old Testament lectionary texts for CSS Publishing Company's magazine *Emphasis;* spoken on Sanctity of Life Sunday for a large Korean church near Washington, D.C.; written a regular column for the newsletter of Presbyterians Pro-Life; and preached in various churches. Retirement has not led to inactivity.

Yet Bud and I are no longer training young women and men in seminary for the ministry of the Word and Sacrament, and we cannot help but wonder at times what the characteristics of seminary graduates will be in the future. Certainly those graduates will partly determine the character of the church for the next decades.

As I look at present seminary education, the picture is not too promising. An experience-based theology has swept through many seminaries, often fostered by the feminist movement. Much contemporary theology has lost its foundation in the scriptures, thus separating itself from the apostolic tradition of the church. The ideology of political correctness, again fostered by the feminists, has altered the liturgy, hymns, and worship of seminary bodies, and that has spread into some of our churches across the land. But such worship has become human-centered, evidenced in the words of many new hymns, and worship has lost its meaning as the praise and service of God. As the church worships, so it will also believe, and the concentration on human beings and not on God bodes ill for the future.

I am encouraged by the fact that some denominational seminaries are bucking the current trends by clinging to the centrality of the scriptures in theology, worship, and ethics. Especially gratifying is the continuation of our work by our son Mark, who is a professor of systematic theology at the Presbyterian Dubuque Theological Seminary in Iowa. Similarly, his wife Katherine is teaching practical theology and serving as a teaching assistant at that seminary. Bud and I feel as if we have passed the torch on to our children, to keep it shining brightly in the midst of the present darkness.

Equally, I find sources of hope for the future in the burgeoning evangelical movement. On college campuses, in seminaries and churches, the evangelicals are clinging to the gospel and, as a result, are attracting thousands of persons to their congregations. Three characteristics threaten their ministries, however. First, there is serious dissension in their ranks over the essentials of the Christian faith. Second, their theology has yet to be set firmly in the context of the Body of Christ which is the church. Thus many of their churches are independent and have little understanding of the one holy catholic church and its traditions through the ages, nor do they feel themselves connected with the whole of God's people in the present, past, and future. They are isolated worshippers sufficient unto themselves.

Third, and perhaps as a result of their isolation and as a cause of their dissensions, the worship, preaching, and theology of the evangelicals is often still understood in terms of propositions and doctrinal correctness. The correctness and truth of Christian doctrine are certainly important, insofar as they mirror the truth of the scriptures. But in actuality, the Bible is not a set of propositions but a story of relationships with God, and mouthing correct doctrine is no substitute for that story or for a living relationship with Jesus Christ. To scorn one's opponents, therefore, because they do not hold correct doctrine is to fail to see the one thing that is needful. Isaiah condemned his people, not because they did not say the proper words, but because their fear of God was learned by rote while their hearts were far from him (Isa. 29:13–14). We evangelicals—and I number myself among them as one called to proclaim the gospel—are finally called to lead our people into a living, day-by-day relationship with God through Jesus Christ and the Spirit, and it is out of that relationship that true doctrine is born.

On the other hand, it must be said that sound doctrine and biblical learning are guides for that relationship, and it is the ignorance of basic Christian doctrine and of the scriptures that I find in the churches. Wherever I go to speak in this country, I find faithful, alive congregations. Many of our churches are healthier than we clergy often give them credit for being. The people in the pews still believe that Jesus Christ is Lord, they still try to live Christian lives, and they still reverence the Bible as the Word of God.

But our lay people also have a great deal of zeal without knowledge. They do not know the content of the scriptures or even where to find most books in the Bible, and they do not know the basic doctrines or beliefs of the Christian faith. As a result, they are "sitting ducks" for any new belief that comes along. They do not have the learning by which they can judge any new religious movement to be true or false, and they do not have the biblical and theological knowledge that can shield them from adopting the fads and follies of alien spiritualities.

Further, because so many of our laity lack theological and biblical discernment, our churches are in danger of losing the Christian faith altogether in one generation. Parents must pass on the language and knowledge of the biblical faith and the traditions of Christian belief and practice to their children, or their children will not be Christians but will fall victim to the hundreds of ideologies and spiritualities that are waiting to include them in their idolatrous folds.

The failure of our laity—and indeed, of many of our pastors—to know as well as to believe is evidence of the church's massive failure in Christian education. Ever since 1903, when the Religious Education Association adopted experience-based learning, à la John Dewey, church school classes for all ages, young and adult, have substituted supposed relevance and inspiration for sound learning, often discussing the social problems of the day with no scriptural basis for judgment about those problems. Everything has depended on "feeling." "How do you feel about this?"—a viral question that still infects many church committees, task forces, and conferences. Add to that the widespread effort to be "sensitive" and "politically correct," and the church's theology and biblical traditions are lost somewhere in the shuffle. To be sure, there are now efforts, at least in the Roman Catholic and Presbyterian Churches, to return to catechetical learning, memorization of biblical passages, and instruction in basic biblical faith and theology. But we have a long way to go before we recover sound learning in the church, thereby laying the supporting foundation for solid faith and practice. Above all else in our time, the church must teach.

Given the turmoil in our mainline denominations and their steady loss of membership, I am often asked what is the future of the church. I have to reply that frankly, I have not the foggiest idea. I do know that God is at work in his church and that the gates of hell, with their ignorance and idolatry, will not prevail against it. Until the kingdom of God comes on earth, there will always be the one holy catholic church because God has promised it (Matt. 16:18). But what shape that church will take is totally unknown to me and to anyone else. The church as we know it in our time may disappear. There may not be a Presbyterian or Episcopal, Methodist or Baptist church anymore. The church, always a minority in the world, may disappear underground, as the church in China and other parts of the Third World sometimes has done. The center of the Christian faith may shift entirely to Third World countries, who are already—God be praised—sending their missionaries to the United States. But until God brings an end to human history in the return of the risen Christ, there will always be a body of believers who worship and serve his name and who wait expectantly for his promised salvation of humankind. God is the Lord of human history and of the natural world; his lordship cannot be overcome but will bring in that time when every knee bows and every tongue confesses that Jesus Christ is Lord, to the glory of God the Father (Phil. 2:10–11).

That is the comfort with which I face the future as I grow older each year. From the promises of my Lord, I know that the turmoil, the evil, and the futility that I see around me in the church and in our society are by no means the last word. God's is the last Word for our life on this planet. He is our Alpha and Omega, the one who created us in the beginning and who will fulfill his good purpose in the end. So I know, as the apostle Paul writes (1 Cor. 15:58), that my meager labors for the Lord—and yours—are not in vain but are part of an ongoing work that God will perfect and use in his purpose.

When you get to be my age, you begin to think occasionally about death, about the inevitable end of all the labors and loves into which you have poured your life. Someone asked Bud and me at a conference one time, "What would you do differently if you had it all to do over?" Neither of us could think of a single thing. We have been blessed, and our course has been guided by God beyond all deserving or expectation.

I take a great deal of satisfaction in our children's character and activities. Not only Mark and Katherine, but also Marie and her husband Paul are contributing significantly to the church. Both of the latter have been ordained as Presbyterian elders and are engaged as leaders of various church activities. We would gladly name our children as our "letters of recommendation" (2 Cor. 3:1), as Paul named the faithful in his church at Corinth. But we would also say with Paul, "Not that we are competent of ourselves to claim anything as coming from us; our competence is from God" (2 Cor. 3:5), and it is he who has nurtured and guided the lives of our children.

I have no illusions about leaving any lasting mark, other than my children's lives, on the world. As the psalmist acknowledges, our days are like grass; we flourish like a flower of the field, but then the wind sweeps over us and we are gone, and no one knows our place anymore (Ps. 103:15–16).

Reinhold Niebuhr illustrated the transitory nature of human life for us one day in class, when he remarked on the statue of a military hero that stood in the courtyard of New York's International House. "Who the hell is Butterfield?" he asked. None of us could remember, though apparently Butterfield had been significant enough in his time to have a statue commemorating him. The wind sweeps over us and we are gone, and no one remembers.

The glad news of the Christian gospel, however, is that God remembers. Another psalmist prays, "Do not cast me off in the time of old age; forsake me not when my strength is spent" (Ps. 71:9). But God does not throw us away in old age or even in death. He remembers us. And our futures, even beyond our death, are bound up with his eternity. The grave is not the door closed forever, the everlasting dark, but the entrance for faith into God's joyous and eternal life. Because Jesus Christ is risen from the grave and lives, he has promised that those who trust in him also shall live (John 11:25–26). From my study of the scriptures and confirmed by his constant guiding of my life, I know that God always keeps his promises.

In the meantime, it seems to me that our one calling is to be faithful in whatever little corner of life God has placed us, to summon will and heart and mind to cling to God in Jesus Christ, to walk the way that he has pointed out to us in his scriptures, and to trust his work with us in all our daily round.

In addition, I think my calling in life is to remind myself with the psalmist, "Bless the LORD, O my soul, and forget not all his benefits" (Ps. 103:2). God has indeed forgiven me my iniquity and redeemed me from the pit of death, as the psalmist sings. The Lord has crowned me with steadfast love and mercy and satisfied me with good all my days (Ps. 103:3–5). From the moment of my conception onward, even to gray hair, he has never forsaken me but has poured out his love upon me. I know that he will continue to guide my steps until he has done all that which he has purposed for me. For that reason, the close of another psalm has always been one of my favorites:

Nevertheless I am continually with thee;
    thou dost hold my right hand.
Thou dost guide me with thy counsel,
    and afterward thou wilt receive me to glory.
Whom have I in heaven but thee?
    And there is nothing on earth that I desire
    besides thee.
My flesh and my heart may fail,
    but God is the strength of my heart and my
    portion for ever.

Psalm 73:23–26